My
Colonial Childhood
in Tanganyika

My
Colonial Childhood
in Tanganyika

For Mary
From Julia with love

Julia Tugendhat

First published in the United Kingdom in 2011
by Julia Tugendhat

ISBN 978–0–9570707–0–7

Produced by The Choir Press

Contents

Chapter 1:	A Virtuous Family	1
Chapter 2	Skeleton in the Cupboard	11
Chapter 3	Destiny	18
Chapter 4	Initiation	25
Chapter 5	Marriage	34
Chapter 6	Dad's Work	45
Chapter 7	DO as Novelist	57
Chapter 8	Mum's Work	65
Chapter 9	Childhood	75
Chapter 10	Stanley and Livingstone	88
Chapter 11	Mwanza	96
Chapter 12	Dar es Salaam	107
Chapter 13	School	112
Chapter 14	The Nuns	120
Chapter 15	Mau Mau	129
Chapter 16	Home	135
Chapter 17	Dislocation	144
Chapter 18	Addendum	154

Acknowledgements

I should like to thank Chrisopher for backing me, John and Ursula Lewis-Barned for their invaluable help and encouragement; Innes Meek for sharing information; my sisters for their forbearance; Claudia Waddams for her editing skills and Ingrid Maggs for a long friendship fostered in Africa.

Dedication

For my grandchildren

Chapter 1

A Virtuous Family

This book tells the story of my childhood in Tanganyika (present day Tanzania), a United Nations Trusteeship Territory that was administered as part of the British Empire. This type of overseas enterprise has long since been consigned to history. I have written it with my grandchildren in mind so that they can get a flavour of a way of life for which they will have no reference points. I start with an apology for its inadequacy. I was woefully uninterested in the extraordinary experiences of my parents while they were alive. How I wish I had asked them more questions. In their turn they did not help matters by travelling so light. They did not leave any papers, records or letters behind them. The African objects they collected can be counted on the fingers of one hand. There is a portrait of our faithful African servant Issa, two elegant wooden figurines that may not even have come from East Africa and a crude stool carved out of ebony which is in my possession. So I have had to scratch at my poor memory, peruse old photos and do some research to get this script together. I hope my older sister Harriet and my younger sister Jane will forgive any errors, artistic licence or missing bits. In his book *Basil Street Blues* the biographer Michael Holroyd has this to say about the search for one's origins. "It is an experience I believe, that possesses many people in these circumstances: to ask questions when it is apparently too late for answers, and then to be forced to discover answers of our own." The answers in this book are my own.

Why did my father choose the colonial administration as a career after reading History at Oriel College, Oxford? A closer look at the family tree which he had so meticulously researched in his retirement, and which at the time I foolishly found so tedious, has since provided some clues. My father came from a professional family whose members combined a sense of public service with an adventurous streak. The oldest paternal relatives I knew as a child were my father's uncles and aunts. These were the offspring of our illustrious ancestor, Henry Austin Dobson (1840-1921). He was born in Plymouth and educated in England and Strasburg. At the age of sixteen he joined the Board of Trade in Whitehall Gardens where he stayed for 45 years. Nobody would have heard of him in this role had he not been a well-known and extremely popular author on the side. His books of lyrical rhyming poetry (which one critic compared to Dresden china) were best sellers. Sevres china would have been a more apt description because his poetry was influenced by medieval forms in French verse from the *triolet, rondeau, ballade* and *villanelle*. Though now out of fashion, volumes like *Vignettes in Rhyme, Proverbs in Porcelain* and *At The Sign of the Lyre,* bound in tooled leather or olive-green bevelled cloth have second-hand value today, largely on account of the delicate illustrations by the artists Hugh Thomson and Bernard Partridge. Austin Dobson was an expert in 18th Century literature and art. He contributed regularly to literary magazines and wrote biographies of Hogarth, Bewick, Fielding, Goldsmith, Steele, Horace Walpole, Fanny Burney and Samuel Richardson. He also produced eight volumes of collected essays which dealt with obscure subjects of this period.

His youngest son Alban became his torch bearer. Alban presented his papers, correspondence and as many editions of his published works as he could lay his hands on to London University Library in 1946. This collection was added to over the years by his son Christopher Dobson and other members of the family. There has been at least one PhD thesis on the work of Austin Dobson but no biography has been written although Alban published a slight volume entitled *Austin Dobson: Some Notes.* Unfortunately Alban avoids personal reminiscences and deals exclusively with the oeuvre. Undoubtedly in this he was honouring his father's own wishes to remain a private person. Austin Dobson revealed very little of himself in his essays or poems. In a memorandum left to his wife and executors he intimated that he was opposed to any kind of memoir. Perhaps he had written enough biographies himself to be familiar with the pitfalls. In his preface to *Austin Dobson* Alban wrote, "I am inclined however to think that the true reason for his desiring to remain unsung was due merely to his excessive modesty, because my father was always prepared to sink into oblivion, and the lines that appear on the last page of his *Complete Poetical Works* represent a perfectly genuine expression of his feelings."

> *But yet, now living, fain were I*
> *That some one then should testify,*
> *Saying, – 'He held his pen in trust*
> *To Art, not serving shame or lust,'*
> *Will none? Then let my memory die*
> *In after days!*

In any event a biographer would have had very little to say. Even his best friend Edmund Gosse had to admit: "Ealing possessed no citizen more regular in his habits or more harmless in his conduct. There was absolutely nothing in his career of over eighty years upon which biography can seize, no glimmer of adventure or faintest tincture of romance." What we know from his correspondence is that he enjoyed a great many literary friendships. He met his first set of writing friends through his work. By chance he was joined at the Board of Trade by Edmund Gosse, Cosmo Monkhouse and Samuel Waddington. The department where they worked was described by a contemporary as "a nest of singing birds." Other literary contacts were made through the Athenaeum, the London Library and the Royal Society of Literature. Austin Dobson knew Rudyard Kipling, Arthur Waugh, Andrew Lang and Oliver Wendell Holmes. His first volume of poems *Vignettes in Rhyme* was dedicated to Anthony Trollope. I have inherited printed copies of two delightful cartoons by Max Beerbohm confirming my great grandfather's literary and social status. One shows Dobson and Gosse composing a ballade in office hours in the Board of Trade being taken unawares by their President Joseph Chamberlain. *The Birthday Surprise* shows the presentation of a bust to Edmund Gosse. Dobson appears alongside G.K. Chesterton, Maurice Baring, Joseph Conrad, and Thomas Hardy among others.

In the poem, *Fame is a Food That Dead Men Eat* there is further proof that Dobson eschewed celebrity and valued his friendships.

But Friendship is a nobler thing,
Of friendship it is good to sing.
For truly, when a man shall end,
He lives in memory of his friend,
Who doth his better part recall,
And of his faults make funeral.

On a few rare occasions Austin Dobson agreed to have his portrait painted. Unfortunately, a portrait painted by G.F. Watts in 1884 has gone missing. Two later portraits were acquired by the National Portrait Gallery: one was painted by Sylvia Gosse, (the daughter of his old friend Sir Edmund Gosse) and the other by Frank Brooks. Photographs of him in later life with thick white hair and droopy walrus moustache do reflect a certain modesty and shyness. He had a large head in relation to his small stature, a feature that cartoonists highlighted. His habits were regular. He would leave for his office at the Board of Trade in the early morning and return to his big house and garden at 75 Eaton Rise, Ealing (pulled down and rebuilt as Cecil Homes) late in the evening. After dinner with the family, he would retire to his study where he would do his writing, research his biographies and answer his correspondence. Considering his full-time career, his literary output was prodigious. He was sometimes accused of being lightweight and a practitioner of *vers de societé* but Edmund Gosse rightly judged the subtlety and skill of his work: "It was a feature of his strenuous modesty, his horror of personal emphasis, and it gives his prose, perhaps, a little less value

Austin Dobson

than his verse, which appears to be, in its own defined field, supreme and without a rival. In verse he rose above his masters, in prose he walked by their side." Austin Dobson also found time to be a devoted and loving father. His children must have enjoyed getting letters from him, especially when they were young because they were peppered with humour and amusing sketches. At one time he had contemplated becoming an artist. He had a talent for drawing and for a time attended art classes in the evening. Instead he took up writing which, despite failing eyesight and rheumatoid arthritis, he was able to do until his death.

Frances Dobson

In 1868 Austin Dobson married Frances Mary, eldest daughter of Nathaniel Beardmore (a distinguished Civil Engineer). She was the forceful partner in the marriage. Her strength and character are obvious in the portrait painted of her. Her grey hair is parted in the middle and scraped back from a handsome square face. Her gaze is direct and her large mouth determined. It seems she could be a termagant. She was an evangelical Christian and a severe and demanding parent. She and Austin produced ten rather remarkable children: five boys and five girls. Frances believed in education for women and saw to it that the girls were schooled to an unusually high standard for the time. As a young woman she herself had written children's books and was a gifted musician. It seems likely that her own intellectual and creative potential was frustrated by her role as mother and wife and she certainly pushed her daughters towards serious careers and pursuits. The boys were steered into the church or public service.

Their oldest son, George Francis Clement was born in 1869. As I explain later he became a missionary and later an ordained priest.

My father, his only son was the oldest grandson of Austin and Frances. The second child, Arthur Dobson was sent to Argentina as an assistant to his uncle James Dobson who was engineer to the Buenos Aires Harbour Board. While there he published an account of an expedition: *Down the Bermejo*. In 1916 he emigrated to Australia where he became an engineer for Sydney Tramways. He met and married Marjorie Caldwell and had two daughters, Ruth and Rosemary. Arthur died when the girls were very young and life for his widow Marjorie became a real struggle but she managed to secure an excellent education for the girls who went on to carve out distinguished careers for themselves. Ruth joined the Diplomatic Service, and became Australia's first woman ambassador; serving in Denmark and Ireland. If the name Dobson has any resonance in today's literary pantheon it is due to the second daughter Rosemary Dobson who is considered to be one of Australia's leading poets. Her output, which includes: *In a Convex Mirror, The Ship of Ice* and *Child with a Cockatoo,* is not large but is highly regarded. The tone is fine and subtle and full of quiet irony and wit. Rosemary married the publisher Alec Bolton.

Austin Dobson's oldest daughter, Augusta Mary Rachel (always known as Mary) was as formidable as her mother who had a strong influence upon her. She became Head Girl of the Princess Helena College in Ealing and won the Evelina scholarship twice. She could have gone to Oxford but chose a musical training instead, becoming the second woman in England to gain a degree in music. Her mother shared her harmony and counterpoint lessons at the Guildhall School of Music. Mary, like her mother, was very religious and this zeal took precedence over her musical talent when she chose to become a missionary in India in 1899. Her aim was to take Christianity to well educated Indian women in Bombay. Although she learnt Gujarati she found converting the Parsis to Christianity an uphill task of twenty-three years. She, and a few like-minded women, did finally succeed in establishing the Missionary Settlement for University Women in Bombay (Mumbai) which now exists as a hostel run by Indians.

Spreading the Christian message became the focus of Mary's life but she found a little time (on the side) to express her creativity. She wrote five books of religious verse and composed religious music. She also produced two moralistic novels: *The Quest of Gervase* and *Earl Osric's Minstrel.* Her last published work *Mount Sinai* was an account of an expedition that she made in 1922 to St Catherine's Convent on Mount Sinai in search of biblical manuscripts. She died in England a year later and was buried in the grave of her parents in Westminster Cemetery, Hanwell. Her friend and fellow missionary Una Saunders wrote a biography of her simply entitled: *Mary Dobson*. It is clear that Mary was bossy, fervent and energetic. These frequently off-putting qualities were fortunately tempered by a gift for friendship and genuine humanity.

The fourth sibling, Grace Lissant was the only one not to go to university. Although she did some travelling, including visits to India and Australia, it was understood that her role was to take care of her parents, a job she committed herself to with saintly dedication until her death in 1953. Ironically she was the only daughter to receive an offer of marriage. The gentleman approached her parents to ask for their permission to marry before consulting Grace herself. The story, as passed down the family is that permission was refused while poor Grace was not informed of the offer. Her younger sister Margaret Bernard (nick-named Daisy) trained as a doctor at the Royal Free Hospital. Austin Dobson spontaneously composed the following lines at the dinner table just before she was due to qualify.

> *When M.B.D takes her Degree*
> *These are the notices you will see:*
> *"If you are feeling low and mean,*
> *Take Dobson's tabloids for the spleen,*
> *For remedies of other class*
> *Take Dobson's hanky-pancreas,*
> *All other remedies but these*
> *Will leave you crippled with disease*
> *Or worse than that, the Royal Free*
> *Will have to write your R.I.P*

She was the most rebellious of the brood and detested her mother. She left home as soon as she could and stopped going to church. Daisy served as a doctor in Egypt during WWI. On her return she qualified as an ophthalmic surgeon and worked at several hospitals and in private practice. She had a wicked sense of humour and was good with children. In fact she would have loved children of her own but never got married. She may have got some consolation from the numerous children she treated for squints in her medical practice. She wrote several medical books. Dorothea de Brissac Dobson known as plain Dorothy graduated from St Andrew's University and became a teacher. In 1921, after a spell as a housemistress at Cheltenham Ladies College, she was appointed Headmistress of Casterton School in Cumbria, made famous by the Bronte sisters who were once pupils there.

In 1820 the Rev: William Carus-Wilson had created a school at Casterton for the children of servants and teachers. Three years later another school was opened for the daughters of the clergy at Cowan Bridge. Charlotte Bronte's bleak description of Jane Eyre's days at Lowood School was based on her own experience at Cowan Bridge. We were told that when Aunt Dorothy first arrived at the school the children were carrying their boots tied round their necks. Presumably this was done to save the leather. A former pupil described her as "extremely neat, caustic and devastating to a fault." By the time of her retirement fifteen years later, the two schools had been amalgamated, academic standards had improved and the finances consolidated. Although Casterton had lost its clerical association it was still noted for its austerity and discipline. Dorothy lived to the ripe old age of 94 and thankfully became more affectionate and tolerant as she grew older.

The youngest daughter, Mildred Eaton, was also a graduate of St Andrew's where she subsequently spent many years as Warden of University Hall. During WWII she volunteered for the Womens' Voluntary Service (WVS). She had a dark moustache and hairs on her chin. She was a forbidding character and we were terrified of her.

The poet Rosemary Dobson wrote a poem about Austin Dobson's five daughters under the slightly disguised title *The Daughters of the Historian*. It gives a flavour of the somewhat oppressive atmosphere in the Dobson household.

The five were decorous. Papa enjoined
That each should offer an original phrase
At dinner-table converse every night.

Governess-schooled, each showed a brilliant mind
And three in turn went out into the world
As teacher, missionary, and almoner.

One died, and one, the youngest, understood
That she should care for frail Mama at home.
None married. Years ahead the three returned.

To school-room conversation, and the nights
Around the dinner-table, cleared and lit,
Sewing small objects for the church bazaar.

The eighth child, Cyril Comyn Dobson followed in the footsteps of his oldest brother Clement. He had a problem with his spine, allegedly caused by being dropped as a baby. After Cambridge he went to Ridley College and became an ordained priest. When he was vicar in Hastings he wrote an interesting pamphlet in support of the theory that Joseph of Arimathea visited Cornwall before setting up house in Glastonbury for some years in the company of his nephew, the child Jesus. Cyril Dobson married and had three children whom I have met at very rare intervals. The ninth sibling Bernard Dobson, won a scholarship to Cambridge and had a very distinguished career in government and the Indian Civil Service, ending up as Financial Commissioner at Lahore.

The last of Austin Dobson's children, Alban Tabor Austin CB CVO CBE had a distinguished career as a civil servant at the Board of Agriculture and Fisheries after attending Emmanuel College Cambridge. His first wife was Katharine Jean Donaldson-Selby and his two children by this marriage, Christopher and Jean, were my father's closest and best-loved cousins. After the death of his first wife Alban married for a second time but had no further children. Following family tradition his son Christopher was educated at Clifton College and Emmanuel College, Cambridge. After serving in WWII as a soldier (and being mentioned in despatches) he was able to indulge his deep passion for books as assistant and then head librarian of the House of Lords. He greatly enhanced this chamber's collection of old books. He was a sweet, scholarly man who was very proud of the family name. He loved scouting around second-hand book shops and barrows and over a lifetime managed to pick up some valuable finds. He built up a fine collection of Austin Dobson's work which was sold at Christie's after his death in 2006. When my parents came home from Africa they bought a house in Kent close to where Christopher and his wife Helen lived with their two children Rosemary and Martin. Our two families became very close. For my father, Christopher was the brother he had never had. Sadly, Martin died young but the cousinly connection is kept alive through Rosemary.

Christopher's younger sister Jean Dobson inherited the Dobson musical talent and a fine contralto voice. She trained first at the Royal Manchester College of Music and then at the Royal Academy of Music. After serving in the Auxiliary Territorial Service in WWII, she became a professional singer and teacher. She gave numerous broadcasts for the BBC and recitals at the Wigmore Hall. With so much artistic and musical talent in the Dobson family I am chagrined that so little seems to have filtered down to me or my children. I wish I had paid more attention to the ten children of Austin Dobson. They were such paragons of virtue and high purpose. What did the boys think about their clever and intellectual sisters? With the exception of poor Grace their careers in education and medicine were on a par. This may have been one reason why they never married. Their mother Frances did not help matters by seeing off any young suitors who came to the house. They might also have been spinster victims of WWI when a generation of young men were wiped out.

Chapter 2

Skeleton in the Cupboard

My grandfather, the oldest of this remarkable tribe had a most interesting life to recount had I been interested enough to listen. Alas, all I can do now is to list the facts and allow them to speak for themselves. Christened George Francis, but always known as Clement, he was born in Kensington and attended St Paul's School in London from which he won an open maths scholarship to Sidney Sussex College, Cambridge. Although he was a scholar and got a First Class degree he decided he wanted to be a missionary rather than an engineer. After studying at Ridley Hall, Cambridge for a further year he joined the Church Missionary Society which sent him out to China. First he lived in Chefoo where he taught the sons of missionaries in the China Inland Mission School. In 1901 he became a master at the Christian Missionary School in Shanghai. As well as Europeans this school took in Chinese boys who could afford the fees. In 1904 the Reverend and Mrs C.J Symonds presided over his marriage in Holy Trinity Cathedral to Janet Blair Neatby, the daughter of a resident physician. My father Kenneth Blair Austin Dobson was born in Shanghai Hospital

Grandpa Clement Dobson

Granny Janet Dobson

on the 5th June 1907. On the family's return to England in 1911 Clement became an ordained priest. After some years as a Curate at St Leonards he was appointed Vicar of St Peter's in Bristol where he remained until 1936. He then became Vicar of Steeple Claydon in Buckinghamshire. During WWII he was enlisted for home duty in the artillery on account of his skill in mathematics.

My sisters and I would see our paternal grandparents intermittently when on home leave from Africa, every three years or so. Granny Dobson was a tall, statuesque, reserved character. Once when we were all staying together in a hotel in Buttermere she asked if she could give Jane, who was a toddler, a bath. Jane, who was her namesake, was her favourite. The bath ended in yells and tears because Jane's back was burnt against the hot tap. Poor Granny Dobson. Being a missionary she probably lived on a higher plane and had most likely never bathed a baby in her life. My father loved her partly because she had done her best to protect him from the ministrations of the formidable Dobson aunts. However, when she died in 1951 I did not miss her because I hardly knew her.

In contrast, Grandpa Dobson was universally loved for his unworldly and eccentric nature. His notorious vagueness obviously irritated Granny Dobson. She recounted how he would set off on expeditions with my father as a young child and come back without him. He came on holiday with us one summer in England when we rented a house in Tarrant Gunville, Dorset. At the time I was obsessed by the sport of butterfly-catching I would pounce on them with a net and then asphyxiate them in a jar containing cotton wool saturated with chloroform which was purchased from the local chemist. I pinned the dead bodies (with wings prettily outstretched) onto a sheet of cardboard. Grandpa Dobson was very upset by this hobby of mine which he regarded as wanton cruelty.

His obsession was altogether more innocent and harmless: he was crazy about trains. His family joked that he had chosen to go to China so that he could ride on the Trans-Siberian Railway. Another oft recounted story about him concerned the Boxer Uprising of 1900. This was a violent attempt by a nationalistic secret society called the Boxers to expel all foreigners from China. The rebels were especially hostile to missionaries. Naturally, Clement's relatives back home were anxious for his safety but the only word received from him during the upheaval was a request for a British Rail timetable. On his return to England he would relax from his parish duties by train-spotting at Bletchley Station.

After suffering a stroke he became bed-bound and was already in a nursing home run by nuns in Eastbourne by the time we left Tanganyika for good in 1957. My father used to take me and my sisters in turn to visit him. He had thick white hair which had once been very dark and piercing almost black eyes under beetling eyebrows. I hated these visits to the urine-saturated ward filled with wheezing and dying old men. I also found Grandpa's behaviour both embarrassing and inexplicable. He would ask Dad to bring him tins, boxes and pieces of string of precise dimensions, though for what purpose was never disclosed. While we were at his bedside he would worry obsessively about catastrophes in the world: an earthquake in India or a mining accident. He would instruct my father to send specific but tiny donations to the survivors. I found this hilarious because he had always been as poor as a church mouse, and cared nothing for possessions. I can now see that his anxiety was coming from a place of goodness and generosity and I am very ashamed of my impatience and mockery.

I wonder what Clement would have made of the skeleton in the family cupboard which Dad didn't unearth until long after his death. My father had always been intrigued by the fact that the Dobson family tree came to a full stop in 1800. The poet Austin Dobson severely discouraged questions about his ancestry. Furthermore it was rumoured that a lot of family papers and correspondence had been consigned to a fire in his garden in Ealing. In his retirement my father spent years and years doing research on the family tree. This entailed visits to Norwich and to

Normandy in France where he and my mother would examine records together. My father broke the taboo of silence by uncovering a French family, a jailbird, and some illegitimate children. He found the revelations more fascinating than dismaying, but they had obviously been deeply threatening to his staid and respectable Victorian forebears.

My father wrote an article of 14,000 words called *Henry Dobson – "Artiste Mecanicien"* in which he recorded the family history which he had so assiduously unearthed. Henry, the *Artiste Mecanicien* came from a Catholic family of artisans. His grandfather, William Dobson (1671-1756) was a carpenter in Bury St. Edmunds in Suffolk. His father, James Dobson, born in 1712, moved to Norwich in Norfolk which, at that time, was an important manufacturing town. There he established a successful business as a carpenter and builder. The *Norwich Mercury* records James's death in the issue of 11 October 1777 as follows: "On Sunday last in the 65th year of his age, Mr James Dobson, many years a considerable carpenter and builder in St. Margarets, departed this life: A man much respected by his acquaintance, having ever discharged the relative duties of society with integrity, honour and approbation." His son, Henry Dobson, was born in 1757 and received his earliest education in France. This was arranged to ensure he received a Catholic education. Henry Dobson married Deborah Carr, the daughter of a dyer and had six children. He earned his living as a builder but was an inventor at heart. He was a member of the United Friars which was a Norwich society for the pursuit of intellectual enquiry. Records show that he read several papers dealing with agricultural inventions to his fellow members.

As Roman Catholics at this time the Dobson family was legally and politically discriminated against. The Catholic Relief Acts of 1778 and 1791 had improved their lot by making it legal for them to practice their religion but until 1829 Catholics were not allowed to hold public office, nor to sit in Parliament. In 1792 Henry Dobson sold his house and possessions in Norwich and emigrated to France with his wife and four of his children. It is a pity that the records are not more forthcoming about his motivation for this move. He might have been irked by the discrimination against Catholics (though his own trade as a builder would not have been affected), or he might simply have been a Francophile. But it was odd that he sold up everything and took his family to France in

1792 when the revolution was in full flood, the Reign of Terror was yet to come and suspicion of foreigners was rife.

"Le Citoyen Dobson" as French archives referred to him did not work as a builder in France but set himself up as an iron manufacturer. Since Britain was ahead of France in industry and manufacture Henry soon found a job. He was employed by a Monsieur de Vandeul to manage some foundries that produced iron products, including cannon for the French army. Henry Dobson became friends with Vandeul's wife Angelique who was the only daughter of the famous French philosopher and encyclopaedist Denis Diderot. Angelique had a high opinion of Henry's ability and character. Eight years later when he quarrelled with Vandeul she defended him in a long letter to her husband. Nevertheless, the rift remained permanent and Henry established his own iron foundry business in Dieppedalle near Rouen where he produced wrought-iron utensils and implements. He was among the first manufacturers to introduce the iron puddling process and to use coal rather than wood in the iron ore process. Henry Dobson therefore made an important contribution to the development of France's industrial history. He did so despite English laws which made it illegal for artisans to work abroad, or to send any machinery or plans out of England.

During this time France and England had been at war. Peace preliminaries had been negotiated in October 1801 so Henry took this opportunity to visit England. His object was not to look up relatives but to learn about new techniques and inventions. Any traveller with such objectives in mind would have been well advised to act with the utmost circumspection. A British subject known to be resident in France was bound to be an object of suspicion. It is inconceivable that Henry Dobson did not know that what he was doing was a treasonable offence. He must have been either foolish or naïve because he was arrested as an industrial spy in Dewsbury Yorkshire in February 1802. Curiously he was caught carrying plans, not for iron but for a woollen factory. Had he succeeded in setting up such a factory in France he might have done very well. Instead, he was charged at the Pontefract Quarter Sessions of the 26th April 1802, with having the plans in his possession with the intention of exporting them abroad. He was sentenced to one year's stay in prison and a fine of £200, and was ordered to stay inside until such fine could be paid. He was imprisoned in York

Castle Prison. When his family in France heard the news, his oldest son appealed to the French government for help with the fine. The Minister of the Interior certainly authorised the payment of the £200 but by the time it arrived Henry Dobson had been charged with a second offence – that of enticing an artificer engaged in manufacture to emigrate to France. He was sentenced to a further year in prison and an additional fine of £500. This time nobody could be found to raise the money.

If at this point Henry Dobson was in despair it would hardly have been surprising. The war had started again, and it might take years for the news of his predicament to reach France; in any case he could not expect the government to come to his aid with money a second time. The case had been reported in various English newspapers but, so far as is known, no relative or friend came to his assistance. Perhaps they believed the stories that he was spying for the French. In fact, the trip seems to have been undertaken at his own expense, and for his own purposes. Some months later he made a bid for freedom. On the night of the 16th May 1803 according to the *York Herald* he made his escape "by means of false keys, having picked the locks and entered through three doors, previous to the place where he was confined, and afterwards scaled the outer walls … by the help of a new rope." He was re-captured two days later and returned to the castle. In the end he languished in prison until June 1807. After his return to France via Holland he never left French shores again and perhaps not surprisingly took formal French citizenship in 1813. He spent his last years working in his own factories with his sons and writing learned articles in the *Annales des Arts et Manufactures* encouraging the use of coal in the iron industry.

Despite his unfortunate experience, Henry sent his oldest son George over to England in 1815 to garner more useful manufacturing information. George liked England so much that he set himself up as a civil engineer, acquired a house, a mistress called Mary and two more children called Elizabeth and James who were christened Dobson in a church in Battersea. History does not relate what happened to these two illegitimate children. Meanwhile, George seems to have abandoned his French wife and five older children in France but he must have kept some communication going because after an interval his oldest, legitimate son George Clarisse joined him. George Clarisse became apprenticed to a well-known civil engineer. Rising up the ladder he became deputy to an able engineer called James Meadows Rendel. In due course he married Augusta Harris who was the sister of Rendel's wife. He ended up working in Holyhead as the Resident Engineer. Unlike his disreputable father, George Clarisse had turned himself into a respectable Protestant Englishman with a conventional marriage and a solid career.

George Clarisse and Augusta's oldest surviving son was Austin Dobson who broke with the family tradition of engineering and became a poet. Three of Austin's four brothers became engineers and Fanny, the only sister, married one. I do not know whether it was George Clarisse himself or Austin Dobson who decided to expunge the French connection from the family annals. In any event, the effect was to cut out two French great-aunts, one great-uncle, three uncles, one aunt and a number of cousins. This seems a great shame. As far as I am concerned the skeleton in the cupboard has added piquancy and unorthodoxy to our high-minded and self-righteous family history. When Dad died in 1981 I found some correspondence with a French woman whom he had addressed as "Chere Cousine." I thought it would be amusing to contact her and arranged a meeting in the Meurice Hotel in Paris. Sadly, the dear cousin was a tight-lipped and graceless character. I got the embarrassing feeling that she thought I was after her money. So ended the intriguing French connection. Too much water had obviously passed under that particular bridge.

The Dobson family burial ground, as far as there is one, is Westminster Cemetery, Hanwell. Here in plot S, Number 7800 is buried Austin Dobson and four other members of the family. The simple gravestone in Portland stone bears a faded inscription to Austin, his wife Frances Mary, Augusta Mary (the musical mission-ary), Katharine Jean Selby Dobson (the first wife of Alban) and Grace Lissant Dobson, the saintly spinster. The sundial placed on the grave has long since disappeared, presumably stolen. It was made from a baluster of old Kew Bridge and used to stand in Austin Dobson's beloved Ealing garden.

Chapter 3

Destiny

With lineage like this, my father, Kenneth Blair Austin Dobson was destined for public service. I know nothing of the first four years of his life which were spent in China but I can imagine him being tenderly cared for by a Chinese *ayi* while his parents went about their missionary duties. Perhaps it was for his sake that his parents decided to return to Britain. There were many health hazards for white children living abroad and fewer educational opportunities. In any event, they ended up living in Bristol where Dad was sent to

Dad, 6 years old

one of the local primary schools. Being an only child of an emotionally distant mother and a father dedicated to parish duties he was probably lonely and self-contained. At the age of thirteen he was sent as a day boy to Clifton College. The education he received in this well-known public school would have contributed to his calling. His uncle Bernard, of Indian Civil Service fame had been a glittering star at Clifton where he had been an exhibitioner, a vaunted athlete and Head of School. He helped pay for my father's school fees. Bernard's younger brother Alban had also been a pupil at the school where he excelled academically and at rugby.

Clifton's motto is S*piritus Intus Alit,* meaning the spirit nourishes within. I notice that the current mission statement of the school includes "implanting moral and spiritual values."

Clifton, with Marlborough, Rugby and some other public schools was well known for producing men who made their careers in the Empire. When my father went to Clifton in 1921 the school was embedded in the values of muscular Christianity, sport, patriotism and community service. The school is proud of its statue of Field Marshal Haig, and old Cliftonians have won seven Victoria Crosses starting with the Boer War. One of its best-known alumni is the patriotic poet and writer Sir Henry Newbolt (1864-1938). His *Vitai, Lampada* inspired by his schooldays at Clifton with its refrain, "Play up! Play up! And play the game!" was at one time known by almost every public schoolboy in England. The poem is about a schoolboy cricketer who grows up to fight for the Empire. Dad could quote chunks from Newbolt's stirring naval poems *Admirals All* and *Drake's Drum* which had been part of the school syllabus. I never heard my father proclaim that his school days were the happiest days of his life, but I never heard him say that they were the worst either. I suspect that he kept his head down and did what was required of him. He did not excel in sport, or become a prefect, but left with good enough academic qualifications to earn a place at Oriel College Oxford where he spent three happy years studying for a history degree. After coming down from Oxford, he applied to join the Colonial Administrative Service.

In order to join the Colonial Civil Service my father had to present himself before a board for a series of interviews designed to probe his suitability. Candidates were usually the sons of professional parents, ex-public school pupils and graduates from Oxford, Cambridge, Dublin or Edinburgh. They did not need to be specialists in science, medicine, or engineering. Expertise was considered less important than character. John Lewis-Barned, a retired colonial civil servant and a friend of my father's was attracted to the service by an article in the *Sunday Express* headed *Sanders of the River, still the best job for a British Boy.* The qualities demanded by the job description were "a sense of vocation, an urge for adventure, and a response to the call of duty, initiative and almost above all, a sense of humour and an ability to return the affection of the people who you are serving." Whatever answers Dad gave to the interviewing board must have passed muster because he was accepted for service in Tanganyika. Despite his Uncle Bernard's distinguished career in India, Dad must have considered that he had a better chance of being accepted into the colonial office than passing the even more demanding Indian Civil Service exam or the separate Foreign Office exam for service in the Sudan. His parents, uncles and aunts were delighted at his career choice which continued the family tradition of service overseas. He had chosen a career that was bound to be interesting, was sufficiently well paid and came with a pension attached. It was also a conventional career path for someone of his education and class.

In the early days colonial administrators had no more than three months formal training and were expected to learn by experience on the job. By 1930 when Dad got his appointment the service had become more professional and candidates had to attend the year-long Tropical African Services Course (known as the 1st Devonshire Course) at either Oxford or Cambridge. Dad stayed on at Oriel College for an extra year while he attended a wide range of practical lectures. By the end he was expected to have a working knowledge of colonial history, agriculture and forestry; tropical

hygiene and sanitation, Swahili, criminal, civil and Muslim law, anthropology, first aid, elementary surveying and field engineering. He was paid £75 (equivalent to £3,750 today) for the first term, £50 for the two subsequent terms and £50 on completion of the course. Dad's means were very limited so the training subsidy would have come in very handy. He was relieved when he passed the exams and the necessary medical checks. He was now entitled to a starting salary of £400 per annum. This was entirely satisfactory to a bachelor of simple tastes like my father.

Dad was given his inoculations and an outfit allowance of £30 to cover the equipment necessary for life in the tropics. F.P. Baker of Golden Square and Griffiths McAlister were the shops that specialised in tropical kit. The most important item was the pith helmet. Invented in the 1840s the cork and pith helmet covered in cloth had become a symbol of the Empire. Belts to protect against cholera and spine pads to ward off sun-stroke had just gone out of fashion. He did require knee-high mosquito boots, a dinner jacket and a raincoat (sewn not gummed). Essential household effects included a mosquito net, a picnic box, a cook's box, aluminium utensils, crockery, glassware, cutlery and linen, pressure and hurricane lamps and a first-aid kit. He had been advised that he could purchase essential items like a hunting rifle and safari tents second-hand in Dar es Salaam. He could also have white and khaki drill shorts, shirts and trousers run up quickly and cheaply on the spot.

It must have been hard for his parents to see him off. They knew that they would not see him again for at least three years but long-distance communications had improved dramatically since his parents were in China and the whole British Empire was now linked by telegraph. The electrical signals that were transmitted through a copper wire were decoded onto flimsy paper at the other end. Mail, which had taken weeks to arrive by sea, began to be carried by aeroplane in the same year as Dad left England. Ship remained the most common form of transport though until after WWII and although the building of the Suez Canal had considerably speeded up the journey to Africa it still took around six weeks.

The Union Castle liner on which my father embarked for Africa in June 1931 made its way down the Portuguese coast and stopped off at Gibraltar where there was nothing else to do but climb the Rock and meet the Barbary apes. There were further stops at Marseilles and Genoa in the Mediterranean Sea. At the head of the Suez Canal there was a statue of Ferdinand de Lesseps to remind voyagers of the Frenchman who had driven through the construction of this canal which had dramatically shortened the journey between Europe and the Orient. Port Said marked the beginning of the East. It was a noisy and exotic port. The passengers lent over the rail to be entertained by skilful conjurors called gully-gully men. On the other side of the ship clustered the bumboats laden with tropical fruits, leather goods, carpets and cheap jewellery for sale.

As the ship continued down the canal past Mount Sinai the heat and humidity grew unbearable. Dad had his first experience of prickly heat to which he was susceptible. Those who had a cabin on the starboard side were much worse off than those on the port side and those, like my father, who were travelling first class, were better off than those in second class. The word POSH which stood for Port Out, Starboard Home, entered the English language as a direct result of these long sea voyages. At Port Sudan passengers could divert themselves with a trip in a glass-bottomed boat for a glimpse of marine life. Aden Harbour was a British haven with Government House, banks, shipping offices and shops. The ship rounded the Horn of Africa and turned south towards Mogadishu where passengers were off-loaded in baskets onto lighters. The next stop was Mombasa in Kenya. This old town featuring Islamic architecture, coral houses and an ancient Portuguese fort perfectly reflected its varied history.

The East African coast, with its natural harbours and strategic trading position, had always been a magnet for foreigners. By the second century AD, Indian and Persian ships were plying regularly along the coastline. Then, from the 7th Century onwards, came Arab traders from Oman who gradually began to settle and inter-marry with the Africans. Islam became the dominant religion on the coast and Swahili, which is a rich mix of Bantu, Arab and Shirazi became the lingua franca of the whole country and beyond. The first Europeans to show a predatory interest in the East African coast were the Portuguese who set up trading posts after Vasco da Gama's historic journey round the Cape of Good Hope in 1498. Some 25 years later these trading stations had been turned into fortified garrisons by the Portuguese who managed to retain control of the coast for two hundred years until Omani Arabs got the upper hand again.

Tanga, which was to play an important part in the future of our family, was the next stop, followed by Zanzibar, an exotic island redolent with history which my parents subsequently visited for the occasional holiday. At this time Zanzibar was the headquarters of the ruling Sultan of Oman. Substantial mansions and palaces occupied by Arabs had been built in the centre. It was hard to imagine that Zanzibar had once been a squalid and filthy place where thousands of slaves were bought and sold. Finally the ship sailed into the lovely palm-fringed sandy curve of Dar es Salaam harbour where iron ships mingled with canoes and Arab dhows. Apart from occasional tedium, the long voyage of six weeks would have helped my father start the physical and mental adjustment necessary for the challenges that awaited him. He had become as acclimatised as he would ever be to the tropical heat. He picked up practical information from the old Africa hands he met on board. He polished up his rudimentary Swahili. And as an unattached bachelor he had a great deal of fun.

Dar es Salaam was the capital of the territory and seat of government. In keeping with tradition Dad was offered hospitality and guidance by a senior officer and an administrative assistant. He was required to sign the Visitors Book at Government House. He next called on the Chief Secretary who formally welcomed him and got him to sign the official Secrets Act. He ordered or purchased goods and clothing that he would need in the outback. Shopping in the single storied shops (*dukas*) that lined the main street gave Dad his first experience of the extraordinary Asian community that managed so much of the infra-structure and trade of Tanganyika.

By the time of Dad's arrival the number of Asians in the territory was expanding rapidly. Most of them had come from India in search of work opportunities. There were several Asian members on the Legislative Council. A growing number were practising barristers, having trained at the Bar in England. They helped build the railways and had opened *dukas* in every corner of the country. They were the traders, tailors, craftsmen (*fundis*), cobblers and technicians. They had real commercial flair and many became millionaires. Although they greatly outnumbered the white population they always occupied a somewhat ambivalent social position between the British, who had political power, and the majority blacks who were the indigenous people. They lived in close-knit communities, guarded their culture and religions and went to separate schools. Some of the Hindu communities built colourful temples. Others belonged to the Ismaili community whose leader was the Aga Khan. The administration would have collapsed without them.

In due course, with all his household goods and baggage laboriously retrieved from the customs shed by the government Passages Agent, Dad set off to take up his post as District Officer in Iringa in the Southern Highlands. The first leg of the journey was by train from Dar to Dodoma. This first train journey made such a huge impression on him that he made this stretch of country the setting for his first novel *The Mail Train*. From Dodoma he travelled in a government lorry 157 miles south along the Great North Road (now called the Tanzam Highway) running from Rhodesia to Kenya. "Great" was a misnomer for the bumpy murram road that threw up clouds of red dust and which took them through miles of monotonous acacia scrub before descending into a steep valley full of ancient baobab trees, the like of which he had never seen. When he reached Iringa there was no turning back. His working life in Africa had started.

Chapter 4

Initiation

By this time my father knew as much as there was to know (at least from a European theoretical perspective) of the history of the territory that was to be his home for the next quarter of a century. The mixed population of Tanganyika was the result of succeeding waves of invaders. The oldest surviving aboriginal people are the Hadza who live in the remote Lake Eyasi region and the Sandawe who live near Kondoa, famed for its ancient rock art. They are the descendants of a much larger community of Bushmen who were pushed out of the way by stronger newcomers. First came Cushite tribes from Ethiopia bringing agriculture and domestic animals with them. They were followed by the Bantu from West Africa. With their strong family and clan structure and their iron tools and weapons they soon became dominant. The Nilotic people moved south from Egypt and the Sudan in the 11th Century and became largely assimilated by the Bantu. The Maasai, who were the next to arrive in the early 19th Century have resolutely kept their own identify, costume and way of life.

In the late 19th Century European explorers and missionaries began to venture into Africa in ad hoc fashion. Some of them were motivated by a strong moral desire to stamp out the slave trade. Others, with commerce in mind, were on the look out for raw materials and new markets for manufactured goods. A few hardy individuals, fascinated by the mystery of the source of the Nile were interested in exploration for its own sake. In due course the British explorers Livingstone, Grant, Speke, Burton, Cameron and Elton discovered the major lakes and rivers of central Africa. Permanent missions and trading posts sprang up in their footsteps. It was then only a matter of time before private enterprises were taken over by governments eager to acquire empires.

Meanwhile German travellers had been doing some exploring of their own. In 1861 Baron Von der Decken reached Mount Kilimanjaro which the German missionary Rebmann had told an unbelieving public he had seen thirteen years earlier. It was Dr Karl Peters who got a stranglehold on the territory. In 1884 he journeyed into the interior and in six weeks concluded twelve treaties with tribesmen whose chiefdoms were then declared to be German territory. In 1885 an international conference held in Berlin formally carved Africa up into spheres of interest. Tanganyika was placed under the protection of the Imperial German Government and was known as German East Africa. Uganda, Kenya (known as British East Africa) and Zanzibar were recognised as British possessions. The Congo, Rwanda and Burundi to the west were de facto in the hands of King Leopold of Belgium.

The native inhabitants of Tanganyika did not take kindly to the German rulers who were so ruthlessly imposed on them. First, the Germans had to put down a coastal rebellion by the Arabs. Then they were engaged in fights with the Chagga, the Wanyamwezi and the Wagogo. The fiercest struggle was mounted by the Wahehe, a warrior tribe living in the vicinity of Iringa. Native resistance was finally and savagely stamped out in 1905 after the *maji-maji* rebellion. This uprising involved many of Tanganyika's tribes and raged with particular violence from the Kilwa region in the east to Songea and the shores of Lake Nyasa in the west. *Maji* means water in Swahili. The witch doctors who had incited the revolt assured the tribesmen that they had the power to turn German bullets into water. Unfortunately this was nonsense: some 100,000 Africans were killed in the fighting and the Germans' subsequent scorched-earth policy led to a three year famine.

The Germans only had a decade of peace in which to rule their colony before WWI started and they found themselves fighting the British in East Africa. At the start of the war in 1914 the British were confident that they would easily overcome the Germans who were heavily outnumbered and surrounded by British and Belgian territory on all sides. But they had reckoned without the cunning and skill of the inspired German commander Colonel Paul Von Lettow-Vorbeck. After a series of daring raids on the Kenya railway Von Lettow resorted to guerrilla tactics and managed to engage an increasing number of British forces right up until the end of the war. With his brave African *askari* and his loyal officers, Von Lettow was reduced to living off the land. He made his own clothing and medicines and acquired munitions in surprise attacks on Portuguese forts on the Mozambique border.

He was never captured or defeated and only reluctantly gave himself up after the Armistice was declared in 1918. General W.F.S Edwards, who received his surrender, allowed him to retain his sword as a sign of respect. While writing this book I stumbled upon a number of curious connections. I have a friend called Hector Hawkins whose uncle was present at this ceremony in Abercorn Northern Rhodesia. Colonel Brian Hawkins recorded his first impression of Von Lettow in the following words: "Instead of the haughty Prussian one had expected to meet, he turned out to be a most courteous and perfectly mannered man: his behaviour throughout his captivity was a model to anyone in such a position." The Germans gave him a hero's welcome on his return home.

In the 1919 Treaty of Versailles Germany lost its African territories to the new League of Nations. German East Africa was renamed Tanganyika and mandated to Britain. Mandate meant that Britain was to rule Tanganyika as a trustee carrying with it a moral obligation to manage the country in the interests of the indigenous people. In this respect the German past record was a mixed one. On the positive side they had poured money into the country and had built an administrative infrastructure which outlasted them. They constructed the railways from Tanga to Moshi, and from Dar to Kigoma as well as a network of roads. They built well landscaped towns containing a court house, a prison, a hospital and government offices (*bomas*) all over the country. They amassed valuable data on the geology and hydrology of the country and set up a scientific and agricultural institute at Amani in the Tanga Province which was said to have cost a great deal of money. Money too had been spent on education, hygiene and agriculture. German missionaries who were encouraged to set up stations in rural areas furthered these services.

On the minus side, the best agricultural land in the northern and southern highlands and along the railway lines had been appropriated for German settlers who produced rubber, sisal, coffee and cotton for export. Those natives who managed to stay on their lands were forced to grow these cash crops, often at the expense of growing their own food. Law and order was maintained through a system of Direct Rule under central control. The German officers exercised control through administrators known as *akidas* who were appointed to carry out their orders and collect taxes. These *akidas* had replaced the traditional chiefs and councils whom the Germans had ceased to trust after the fierce resistance they had initially encountered. The *akidas* were often Muslims of Arab or Swahili origin and were unpopular.

In the end, any benefits the Africans might have experienced under German rule were wiped out during the 1914-1918 military campaign. The war had a disastrous effect on the country. According to Edward Paice in his instructive book *Tip & Run*, 45,000 African soldiers and bearers died in the campaign, many of them as a result of poor medical and sanitary facilities. With so many men enlisted in the fighting, the agricultural smallholdings called *shambas* were left untended. This neglect, combined with a drought in 1917 led to a severe famine. Then, to top it all, there was an epidemic of Spanish flu which the Africans called "a great darkness." No proper records were kept of the number of Africans who were conscripted or who died from illness or starvation afterwards. Neither did German or British officials ever acknowledge the unjustifiable losses or apologise for them.

The first task of the British government was to organise the repatriation of German settlers and the sale of their estates and lands, many of which were bought by Indian and Greek traders. They took over much of the German administrative machinery and continued the system of Direct Rule until the arrival of Sir Donald Cameron as Governor in 1926. He introduced the system known as Indirect Rule which had been successfully implemented in Nigeria. In essence, this meant that colonial rule was to be exercised through the tribal chiefs. It was impractical in some areas but by and large the British introduced good settled administration over most of the country, with the traditional leaders of the indigenous peoples as their spokesmen. In theory, the District Officer was now legally the adviser to the Native Authorities in his district. The advice that he offered was still tantamount to an order but there was a subtle shift of emphasis in favour of the natives. By Order in Council 1920 the aim of the administration was to help the Africans develop the skills and knowledge to enable them to govern themselves. Indirect rule was also a practical solution to the problem of governing a huge area by a small number of British administrators without allowing whites to settle large tracts of land as had happened in Kenya. When my father arrived in 1931 Indirect Rule was functioning but Tanganyika was still a poor agricultural territory which received minimal investment and resources from home.

If my father had been asked at the beginning of his career how long he thought it would be before Africans could rule themselves he would have said that he would not live to see it. This was a generally held opinion in the administration. In 1931 the Legislative Council, created to advise the Governor was conspicuous for the lack of a single African representative. *The Handbook of Tanganyika* printed in 1930 explained the deficit as follows: "It is contemplated that a proportion of the seats will be reserved for Africans when suitable persons become available, but there is not yet an African with sufficient command of the English language or with general education who could be appointed to take part in the deliberations of the Council."

Dad strongly adhered to the principles of mandate and Indirect Rule. He also accepted the ethos of the colonial service which slotted in easily with the lessons of his upbringing and public school. In his book, *Once a District Officer,* Kenneth Bradley describes this culture perfectly. "We were committed to one of those professions where, as in the Church or in teaching, dedication is essential and brings its own reward. We were there to serve and not for profit, for there was none, unless you felt like going out to shoot a couple of elephant once a year on your game licence. We were absolutely forbidden to touch politics, such as they were, or to own land, or to engage in commerce, or to be involved in any way. In the Service, the only spur was promotion with its promise of more pay and more allowances, a better house or a bigger station."

Iringa was a perfect first posting. In addition to its spectacular position at the top of an escarpment overlooking the Little Ruaha River, and its cool climate, Iringa had a sizeable European community. The town was founded by the Germans who had erected stout stone buildings with attractive tiled roofs. The *boma* resembled a cloistered monastery. In this and every *boma* in the country emblems of Empire were on show. A photo of King George V hung on the wall. In the courtyard the Union flag would be lowered at sunset and raised at dawn. The prison – dubbed His Majesty's Hotel – was near by.

The lively social life – focussing on the sports club – was leavened by the presence of white farmers who grew tobacco, crops and vegetables. I have a few black and white photos dated 1931 which are stuck in a mouldy black album: one photo shows a large group of Europeans gathered to celebrate the erection of a war memorial to the Germans killed in the war; the men are dressed in khaki or white suits and solar topees. There would have been many Germans amongst the participants. Some had remained during the war while others trickled back afterwards to farm, trade and run hotels.

Another photo shows a tiny white-washed mud bungalow with a primitive doorway flanked by four uneven windows – two on each side. The caption for this is ADO's house. As my father was Assistant District Officer this must have been his first home in Africa. Hopefully, as a young bachelor he didn't have to do much more than sleep in it because it looks very basic indeed. In other photos Dad, looking handsome and relaxed, is pictured with European friends and colleagues, drinking on verandas, sheltering under a canvas tent and posing with a Ford car. The Kitonga Pass where the river widens into a flat pool features as a popular place for picnics and occasional trout fishing. The German mission at Tabaga seems to have been a favourite place to visit. The club which was the hub of ex-pat social life had tennis and golf facilities. A whole page is taken up with photos of a mongrel puppy called Jean. This was the first of many beloved Dobson dogs.

There are pictures of the *askaris* and office messengers and of local natives who wore toga-like garments and shaved their heads. The local Hehe tribe was proud of its culture and history which quite recently had included fierce resistance to German occupation. Their charismatic chief Mkwawa had not been forgotten. During the rebellion he had ambushed a German war party, killing most of the troops. He managed to evade the Germans for four years and, in the end, rather than be captured had committed suicide. His head was severed and sent back to the Reich in Germany. Long after my father had left Iringa, the skull was restored to his tribe in a great ceremony and was buried with elephant tusks at the head and feet as befits an important chief. Sir Edward Twining, the Governor whose tenure spanned much of my father's career had managed to track it down in the Bremen Anthropological Museum and led the negotiations for its restoration. Mkwawa is a folk hero in Tanzania to this day.

By the beginning of 1933 Dad was living in Mbeya – which lay further south near the border with Rhodesia. Mbeya, which is Tanzania's fifth largest city today, was at that time a small new settlement built to service a gold mine in Chunya. It had a fabulous setting in the southern highlands; part of the Rift Valley, these are studded with dormant volcanic peaks, crater lakes, tracts of indigenous forest, rivers and waterfalls. The rains produced ravishing displays of wild orchids and proteas. By this time Dad had acquired a new black and white dog and a new set of European friends, including a few young children. The weekly arrival of a tiny plane at the rudimentary aerodrome must have been one of the highlights of the week. There are ten photographs of aeroplanes which look as if they are constructed from matchsticks. Run by Imperial Airways they transported mail and essentials and must have been objects of wonder and curiosity to Africans and Europeans alike.

Other photos illustrate something of Dad's working life: there are pictures of him on safari under canvas with a colleague, the car he either owned or used is usually stuck in mud or a raging torrent, there are photos of Africans clearing out the bush, constructing roads, and building bridges under his watchful eye.

From these bits and pieces I think it safe to assume that Dad's first tour in Africa was challenging, varied, instructive and enjoyable. He had worked very hard to achieve some necessary objectives. He passed his first oral exam in Swahili. He had got through his probationary period as a cadet and was confirmed as a permanent colonial civil servant with a pension and a rise in salary. He was now entitled to wear a white dress uniform and sword on ceremonial occasions. More importantly, he was free to find a wife. At this time DOs were only allowed to bring wives back with them when they had finished their probationary tour.

District Officer

Chapter 5

Marriage

The woman Dad found was Evelyn Barbara Phillips who proved ideally suited to share his life in the wilderness. On her father's side my mother was descended from a strict non-conformist family who, for generations, had been involved in the Congregational Church of Sherwell in Plymouth. Early in the 20th Century several family members left the tightly-knit Sherwell church community and dispersed to Bristol, London and Liverpool in the service of trade and family business. My mother's grandfather headed up a branch of the family in Liverpool. He was called Louis Bartlett Phillips, was married to Ellen Sophia Pillman, and ran the Liverpool branch of a flour importing business called Pillman and Phillips. Of Louis Bartlett Phillips' five children only one married and had children and that was my mother's father. Daisy, the eldest daughter died unmarried at the age of twenty. The second child Evelyn, known to us as Auntie Evie remained a spinster until she died in 1956. When I knew her she was very thin, possibly anorexic and lived a lonely life with a companion in an overheated flat in Liverpool. Her younger brother Uncle Harold was more cheerful and drove a dashing old Bentley car but remained a bachelor all his life. The youngest son Joseph (always known as Alex) went missing on the Somme and was presumed dead in 1917. My mother's father David Allison Phillips had thirteen first cousins. Only two out of these got married. My grandfather married May Elsie McBride from Belfast, broke away from the family business and joined a cotton broking firm. They lived at 22 Ivanhoe Road before moving to a large Victorian house called Clonterbrook in St Anne's Road in a middle-class suburb of Liverpool.

The Phillips family, while manifestly worthy, was not particularly distinguished. They did however lay claim to one famous ancestor. This was the Liberal MP Samuel Plimsoll (1824-1898) after whom the Plimsoll line was named. We would joke about him as children. Plimsoll, known as "The Sailor's Friend" took up the cause of coffin ships in parliament. These were trading ships which, over-insured and over-loaded frequently sank with terrible loss of life. Thanks largely to the untiring efforts of Samuel Plimsoll MP a Royal Commission on unseaworthy ships was set up. In 1876 the United Kingdom Merchant Shipping Act made the load line (still known as the Plimsoll line) compulsory. Mum was amused that the common-or-garden plimsoll with its rubberized sole to prevent slippage on board ship was also named after her so-called ancestor. He sounds like a good chap to have as a forbear but the connection is very tenuous indeed. Samuel was David Phillips' great grand-mother's nephew through her sister's marriage to Thomas Plimsoll.

My grandfather was quiet and reserved and as children we were in awe of him. He was thin and tall and had a pointy nose and a balding head of hair. He was a model citizen and a serious Christian. It was said of him that he could not tell a lie. He was involved with Sefton Park Presbyterian Church which he attended regularly. When he died a plaque was erected in the church which read:

> David Allison Phillips. Born 7th October 1880. Died 5th December 1958. For 45 years he served this church as Deacon, Elder, Session Clerk & Treasurer. He was a good man – "Peace, peace, he is not dead, he doth not sleep/ He hath awakened from the dream of life."

In the first quarterly magazine of the church printed in 1959 the Reverend William Sutherland paid a tribute to my grandfather which accords well with what I knew of him. He said that he was a good man, in the biblical sense of combining inward truth and sincerity with outward usefulness and efficiency. "In the business affairs of the Church he showed great capacity and soundness of judgment. His penetrating judgment and his extreme scrupulous-ness allied with charitableness in speech, all combined to make his judgment extremely reliable." Sutherland went on to say that David Phillips shrank from publicity and prominence in public affairs and that it was only his strong sense of duty that impelled him to take office in the Church. His health, which was always delicate, stopped him joining up in WWI but he served as a Special

Constable. He involved himself in many good causes, including the Hyslop Street Boys' Club. Sadly, the church, plaque and all, as well as the grave have since been destroyed and the area developed. However there is a family monument in Section GEN H. No 96 in Toxteth cemetery. A granite grave containing a large stone cross is surmounted by four ascending slabs of stone. On all four sides of these are inscribed the names of Louis Bartlett, his wife Ellen and their six children. Grandpa Phillips' name has been added and although the ashes of May Elsie are interred elsewhere her name has been included on the monument. An upright granite stone has recently been laid on top of the slabs to take the names of my mother's youngest brother Harold Leslie Phillips and his wife Constance.

Granny Phillips, a lively extrovert was a perfect contrast to her sober husband. May Elsie McBride came from a Scottish Protestant family in Northern Ireland. Her father Samuel McBride was a prosperous linen merchant who was head of the family firm Robert McBride and Co: She had a sister and three brothers. The siblings were constantly at odds with each other. May Elsie did try to mediate between them, but in the end she too caused offence and gave up trying. I did once meet my grandmother's oldest brother Dr Ernest McBride who was Professor of Zoology at Imperial College in London and a Fellow of the Royal Society. David Phillips met Elsie McBride when he was visiting Belfast on business. Their wedding reception was held at home at Edgehill, Lennoxvale. From an old photograph it is clear that the house was large and comfortable with an enormous garden containing a pond.

Granny Phillips claimed descent from the illustrious Sir John Moore who was killed in 1809 during the defence of Corunna. Mum recalled being taken on a family holiday all the way to Spain to see his monument. An exhausting climb in the blazing sun made an impression on her. The original monument had been a handsome wooden edifice erected by a Spanish general on the site of Moore's grave. It was later replaced by the stone monument my mother toiled her way up to see. Despite my efforts to find a link, and those of my father before me, the connection seems to be apocryphal.

Granny Phillips was small and round. She had thick brown curly hair and shrewd blue eyes. She had gone to finishing school in Dresden, spoke German and was a talented musician. Had she lived in a different era she might well have become a professional violinist. I never saw her play the violin but she had a fine singing voice. She had a fund of Irishisms like "sit down off your feet,"' cautionary tales and funny songs. One of our favourites was about a previous suitor whose surname was supposedly Ramsbottom. Granny Phillips swore that she turned him down with the words, "I can't marry you because I don't want to be called Sheepsbottom and my children the Lambsbottoms." We never grew tired of her song recitals which tended to have a dark side. A typical example was, "Willy in a football jersey fell into the river Mersey. Ring me up at Birkenhead when you get there father said." 'There were Three Boys of Bristol City" was another favourite sea shanty. Three feckless youths called gorging Jack, Guzzling Jimmy and the Little-One Billy took a ship out to sea. When they ran out of food at the equator they decided to eat the hapless Billy. Granny's voice would rise in raucous relish on the line, "We have no food we must eat HE."

The wedding photo of my grandparents is telling; David looks as if he is going to a funeral while May Elsie looks happy. They were devoted to each other, but fifty years of marriage to such a puritan and religious man were restrictive: there was no television in the house and films were forbidden. After David's death in 1958 May

Granny Elsie Phillips & Grandpa David Phillips

Elsie began to kick up her heels. She wasted little time in selling Clonterbrook and moving into a mansion flat in which the television had pride of place. She became an avid filmgoer and saw *Gigi* seven times. She took up bridge and had a full social life with family and friends. Towards the end of her life she reluctantly left Liverpool and moved to Keston village in Kent where we had settled. I enjoyed visiting her in the Barn House where she lived with my favourite aunt Molly but as a child we had lived too far apart to have built a relationship and as a young adult in the 60s I was too busy to consolidate it. She died in 1967 and was cremated in Beckenham Crematorium.

David and Elsie May Phillips had four children. The oldest was Mary Eleanor always known as Molly. Denis was next, followed by my mother Evelyn who was born in Liverpool on 3rd June 1912. The youngest boy was christened Harold but was always called Leslie. If you were prosperous, middle-class and lived in the right area, Liverpool was a splendid place in which to grow up between the wars. I never heard my mother call herself a *Scouser* but she was proud of being a *Liverpudlian*. Liverpool had grown rich on the profits of trade and slavery. As it expanded through the centuries the city acquired magnificent civic buildings: the Town Hall, St George's Hall, the Royal Liver building, huge dock complexes, numerous churches and two Cathedrals. The cultural heritage which, in my day in the 60s spawned the Beatles and the poets Roger McCough, Adrian Henry and Brian Patten had always been strong in Liverpool. As my mother grew up she had access to concerts, theatres and museums.

The area around Sefton Park and Aigburth Road provided plenty of activities for the four children who got on well at this stage. They were all great teasers and gave each other nicknames. Molly was Potty, Denis Bozo, Mum was Bib and Leslie Boko. They called their mother "Missis" and referred to her as "the belle of Belfast." They lived within walking distance of Sefton Park with its lake, palm house and statues. Mum took to riding in a big way: she was taught in a local riding school and trotted out in Sefton Park's Rotten Row. There was boating on the big lake in summer and skating when it froze over in winter. They all learnt to play tennis and to swim. They used to go as a family on climbing holidays in Devon, Wales and Cumbria. They were educated in local schools until it was time for the girls to be sent to board at Harrogate College and the boys at Sedburgh.

Mum and Molly enjoyed Harrogate where they did well academically. Mum was encouraged to continue her riding activities in a local riding school and competed in horse shows. The girls grew into glamorous, good-looking young adults and to their father's distress, led a racy social life with a smart Liverpool set. Despite the slump in the early thirties this set was determined to have a good time. Molly and Mum were in the height of fashion: they wore cropped hair, smoked cigarettes, played bridge,

drank and danced in the famous Adelphi Hotel. One of the most popular events in their social calendar was The Grand National at Aintree. Mum and Molly would organise large parties of friends for the event. Mum, who had become an intrepid horse woman, took every opportunity she could to go hunting in the surrounding countryside and in Ireland. One of the few possessions she brought to Africa from England were her knee-high brown leather hunting boots which were kept in shape by wooden stays and followed her wherever she moved.

The two girls in the family were more intellectual than the boys who were expected to go into the family business rather than university. Molly had ambitions to go to Oxford University but had to shelve them when she contracted tuberculosis. Instead she spent a year at a clinic in Switzerland taking the cure which largely consisted of sitting outside on the terrace, wrapped in blankets breathing in the mountain air. On her return she got married to a very dashing young man who sported a black moustache and looked like Clark Cable. His name was Charles Robert Cope but we always knew him as Uncle Bobby. They had one adopted daughter called Victoria. Denis first married Anne Harrington, and then years later Lucy Joad, but remained childless. Leslie married Constance Lloyd who produced Sandra and Mark. We would reunite with these uncles, aunts and three cousins every time we returned to Liverpool on leave.

My mother ended up being the only sibling to go to university. Her first experience at Liverpool University where she studied classics was not a success. She liked neither the institution nor the subject. And her social life was made unbearable by a male stalker. She took stock, and decided that because of her love of animals she would be better off doing a diploma course in Agriculture and Food at the University of Reading. In the event, this course, which she did not complete, proved highly relevant to her future life in Africa.

My mother and father first saw each other on Paddington Station. It was love at first sight for them both. Even as a fairly young child I think I knew that both my parents were extremely good-looking. I probably overheard people talking about them. It was a family joke that someone had called my father "Barbara's golden haired Adonis." As a teenager I knew for sure. My father was slender and tall (well over six feet). He had classic features with a broad brow, neat ears, a good mouth and strong chin. He had thick wavy brown hair which he never lost. He kept it glossy and tidy with brilliantine. My mother was sultry-looking. She had short dark curly hair, a slightly oriental slant to her eyes, a beautiful straight nose and full sexy lips. Their personalities were complimentary. My father was quiet, reserved and thoughtful. He kept a cap on his emotions and was cautious in his decisions: he was a model of moral rectitude and could not dissemble. My mother was lively, quick and impetuous. She also had a lightening temper. In different ways they both had that most elusive of qualities – charm. When my father spotted Mum on the station platform she was wearing a tartan beret and was pulling an undisciplined terrier along on a lead. Dad followed her on to the train and started up a conversation about her dog. Anyone knowing my father well would have been astonished by his forwardness. The bold approach paid off because, after a short courtship, she agreed to drop out of university and follow him back to Tanganyika to get married.

When she went out in the autumn of 1934 accompanied by her

mother (and an old school friend called Nan Nicholas) she made the journey by an Imperial Airways Short Sunderland Flying boat. This was quite a daring thing to do: commercial air travel was in its infancy and none of them had flown before. The plane was one of the S.23 series Empire boats. Forty-two of these were built for commercial service and were known as the Cs because each was given a name beginning with C. The first, christened *Canopus* had its debut in July 1931. It had a maximum speed of 320mph and could accommodate 5 crew members and 17 passengers. The cabin was not pressurized, the noise of the propellers was deafening and there was no heating. Earache and airsickness were inevitable. The flying boat took off from Poole Harbour, landing for the first night at Marseilles. The following day it crossed the Mediterranean, stopping at Augusta where passengers could partake of a leisurely lunch. The second night's stop was Alexandria and third was on the Nile at Cairo. Here the plane broke down. Mum, desperate not to miss her own wedding, managed to hitch the party a lift to Dar es Salaam on a private plane. On their arrival in the capital their extraordinary travels were not yet over. They now had to take a train to reach Dodoma where the marriage was to take place.

Mum's first African train experience would have been astonishing. This was a train that little boys dream of: it was made of wood and metal and was pulled by a huge black and red Garratt

locomotive with gleaming brass fittings. The heat in the carriages, the red dust pouring in through the window cracks and the swarms of flies must have been overwhelming. Wild game, which today is largely confined to nature reserves, was plentiful and still freely roamed across uncultivated land. Mum would have wondered at the sight of zebra, giraffe, antelope, hartebeest, Grant's and Thomson's gazelle as well as ostrich, vultures, bustards, kites and secretary birds. She was to become a serious bird watcher and had illustrated books at hand to help her to identify the new and exotic species of plants, animals and birds that she was seeing for the first time. Mum learnt to love the austere beauty of the desolate central bush plateau studded with acacia scrub, random giant boulders and weirdly shaped red anthills. Villages, consisting of clusters of round huts with pointed thatch roofs, were few and far between. Occasionally she saw naked *totos* (little children) waving at the train as it chugged past and the odd *bibi* (mother) wrapped in a brightly printed cotton cloth with a baby tucked round her back and a huge load on her head walking steadily and gracefully as if to nowhere.

Dodoma, which is the nominal capital of Tanzania today, must have looked small, poor, and insignificant in comparison with Harrogate and Liverpool, but it had been an important town under German rule. The name Dodoma derives from *Idodomya* meaning the Place of Sinking. The name commemorates a local clan who ate their neighbours' cattle, then placed the dismembered tails in the swamp to try to convince the owners that their missing beasts had died by drowning. History does not relate whether this ruse worked. The town contained some Indian *dukas,* the *boma,* the Railway Hotel, a hospital, and the sports club.

On 31 October 1934 my parents were married in the Cathedral of the Holy Spirit. My mother wore a simple, long, white dress and floppy hat which she had brought with her as part of a specially prepared tropical trousseau. In one of the wedding photographs it is clear that my father had holes in the soles of his shoes. The wedding party included a diminutive clergyman, the two visitors from England and a handful of Dad's local friends. It is unlikely that they had a honeymoon. By this time my father had been appointed Assistant District Officer, Kwimba which was a small settlement in an isolated region in the middle of Lake Province. He was transferred to Maswa shortly afterwards.

Here in the outback my sophisticated, essentially urbanite

mother spent her first two years of married life. She had certainly
been thrown in at the deep end. Her first home would have been
the most basic of the government houses and she would have had
to rely on a handful of Europeans for company. Maswa was a district
of rolling wooded country with thin populations. It was essentially
cattle country and many of the administrative problems involved
cattle. The local people, the Sukuma, had continuous trouble from
Maasai cattle-raiders who were not averse to using violence. The
veterinary department was working hard to eliminate rinderpest
which was a killer disease for cattle. Another killer disease was
tsetse fly which could only be controlled by clearing bush. There
were areas of good land which only needed water to enable people
to live there. Roads had to be built and dams excavated.

Mum and Dad would have dropped in to see the Leakeys who
were hard at work on their archaeological site in the Olduvai
Gorge. Louis Leakey, the son of English missionaries in Kenya, was
an archaeologist who was to have an immense impact on the history
of Tanganyika as well as the history of mankind. He came to
excavate the ancient fossil beds of the Olduvai (present day
Oldupai) Gorge in 1931. Five years later he married Mary Nicol
who was a gifted amateur archaeologist. So began a partnership
that changed the then current theory of man's evolution. Mary,
who was probably the better scientist, shot to fame with the

discovery of the skull of *Proconsul* in 1948. Eleven years later she discovered *Australopithecus Boisei*. Dad had long since left Africa when Louis again hit the news with his discovery of *Homo Habilis*. Mary continued to work and live in Olduvai after her marriage to Louis broke up and was rewarded with the most spectacular find of all – the 3.6 million year-old Laetoli footprints. These have had to be covered up for the sake of preservation but their casts can be seen in the Oldupai Gorge Museum.

As yet unencumbered by babies my mother went on safari with my father. There was so much to love and so much to hate in Africa. Mosquitoes, ants, flies, spiders and other creepy-crawlies were a menace but the wildlife was spectacular. The large tracts of land which were not used for grazing or crops were home to elephant and other wild animals. Maswa was within reach of the Ngorongoro crater and the Serengeti plain. This area was not yet a conservation World Heritage site so campers could alight at will and Maasai herdsmen grazed their cattle on the plain amidst the wild animals. The seasonal migration of stampeding wildebeest was an unforget-table sight. Life might be tough and basic but it was never dull. And that was the essence of its appeal to my mother who was a born adventurer.

Taking to Africa

Chapter 6

Dad's Work

Dad was critical of the policy whereby District Officers were frequently moved from one station to another. His career pattern was typical. After his probationary tour in the Southern Highlands he was sent to hardship posts in Kwimba and Maswa. In 1937 he was transferred to Korogwe and then Lushoto in the north – east of the country. He spent rather longer than usual in this posting because there was no home leave for the duration of WWII. 1942 found him in Ngara on the Belgian-Congo border; 1944 in Biharamulo; 1949 in Mwanza and 1955 in Dar es Salaam. I too find the logic of these frequent dislocations puzzling. The postings were in districts with very different tribes, languages, customs, climatic conditions and agricultural problems. No sooner was a DO familiar with his patch than he was moved to another and had to start over.

As a cadet DO, Dad was at the very bottom of the pecking order. At the top was the Governor who made the laws with the advice and consent of the Legislative Council. The Secretariat was made up of administrative departments: customs, education, finance, justice, lands, surveys, mines, public health, police, prisons, post & telegraphs, public works, railways, veterinary, geological survey and agriculture. The territory was divided into eight provinces run by Provincial Commissioners. The provinces were sub-divided into districts run by District Commissioners with District Officers under them. Altogether, some 200 British administrators, with the assistance of auxiliary staff, were responsible for running a country the size of Germany, France and Belgium put together. The native population in 1936 was under 5 million. There were approximately 6,000 Europeans and 16,000 Asians. Two-thirds of the country was uninhabited.

In theory, my father would have known what the main thrust of his task was. He had to get to know the district, its people, its leaders and its problems as soon as possible. He had to make sure that the poll tax was fairly and properly collected because it paid for both central and native administration. He had to maintain law and order which meant many hours in the court room adjudicating cases that were beyond the remit of native courts, and he had to make sure that all the interlocking departments did their work properly. There was only one sure way of getting to know the district and that was to go on safari which would be a key feature of his work in every district.

By the 1930s more ground could be covered by the use of motor vehicles. Dad was accompanied on safari by small retinue consisting of a messenger from the *boma* who acted as his eyes and ears, a house servant and porters to carry the tent and provisions. Sometimes a sheep or cow was taken along to provide meat. He would stop in every village where the women would welcome him

Snake Dance

with ululating song. He would be received by the local chief with great ceremony and sometimes with gifts of eggs, vegetables and fermented palm wine called *pombe*. Africans love to talk and it was rude to be in a hurry. There might also be a *baraza* where the village elders would meet with the DO for a leisurely discussion of local affairs. Sometimes he would be entertained with an *ngoma* (music and dancing). Every tribe had its own rituals and costumes for these *ngomas*. The dancers were decorated in body paint, brass bangles and fancy headdresses. The drumming, dancing and drinking would go on all night. Some tribes danced with bells round their ankles, some with pythons in their arms and others with boxes under their feet. The dancing could be so intense and drawn-out that the participants entered trance states. Dad found safaris exhausting but satisfying and began to enjoy them more when he was able to take my mother along as a companion. They appreciated the relaxing moments at the end of a hard day when they were able to relax in their canvas chairs. A whiskey or gin and tonic at sundown with the smell of cooking in the air was wonderfully reviving. Dad wasn't a natural or keen hunter. He didn't really like shooting for its own sake but stalking a guinea fowl or a small deer for the pot was a different matter.

Dad would spend time with significant people in the village and then go through the tax accounts and books. Gradually he would build up a picture of the general state of affairs in his district, the crop yield, tax collection problems, the extent of any damage done by locusts, drought, floods, tsetse fly or the plague. It was important not to miss anything, especially in the matter of audit because in those days officers could be surcharged by the Government for inefficiency or oversight, and the money deducted from their salaries. He checked up on work initiated by other departments such as road or building works, land clearance to eliminate the tsetse fly or agricultural schemes to stem soil erosion. Invariably there were *shauris* (disputes) to sort out in the court house. These might involve a runaway wife or a dispute about land ownership. On one occasion he hunted down and shot a man-eating lion which had been terrorising a village.

Court work took up a great deal of time. All administrative officers were ex-officio magistrates. (Professional magistrates were restricted to judging capital crimes and appeals). Dad learnt quickly on the job and being a fair-minded person is likely to have made the right judgments most of the time. His view was that a good dose of common sense and a pragmatic approach were as important as knowledge of the law. All the while, Dad was practising and improving his Swahili. He passed two official exams at lower and higher standard (a requirement to stay in the service) during his first five years in Tanganyika. He also progressed in the judicial system as he gained experience in the administration of local justice. In 1942 he was given the jurisdiction of First Class Magistrate which meant that he could try cases which carried more severe penalties in the form of fines, strokes or up to two years imprisonment.

Missionaries also played an important role in Tanganyika although their contribution was more controversial. Dad was a great admirer of Dr David Livingstone, the celebrated Scottish missionary explorer who spent years in Tanganyika looking for the source of the Nile. Christian missionary activities started as the result of Livingstone's call to Oxford and Cambridge in 1857 to join in making Africa "free, civilized and Christian," an appeal which led to the creation of the Anglican Universities Mission to Central Africa. Famine, war and fever put an end to the early attempts to establish permanent missions until eventually a station was established in the district of Tanga. More followed, including one on Lake Nyasa. Not to be outdone, the Roman Catholics were quick to do the same. The Holy Ghost Fathers secured a site for their church in Bagamoyo. They built a school and a hospital and began farming on a large scale. In time, they had established a chain of missionary posts which stretched from the coast to Lake Tanganyika. In 1878 a party of missionaries of the Societé des Missionnaires de Notre Dame of Algeria arrived. They became known as the White Fathers because of their long white garments. With the awakening of German interest in Tanganyika came a rush of Protestant and Lutheran missions. The first was the Benedictine Order of St. Ottilien from Bavaria. Their evangelising took place around Dar es Salaam where in 1897 they built the handsome edifice now known as St Joseph's Cathedral. By 1914 there were few areas which were not served by missions of one denomination or another.

Dad had personal friends amongst the missionaries. He admired their record as intrepid pioneers and explorers and valued the ancillary services such as medicine and education that they offered, especially in the wilderness. But he felt more dubious about their zeal to convert the Africans to Christianity. Mission children invariably became alienated from their families and culture. Clashes between a district officer and the head of a mission were not uncommon. District officers were at pains to allow the natives to follow their customs without undue interference whereas some missionaries thought it their duty to stop polygamy, combat the power of witch doctors and discourage puberty rituals like female circumcision.

The war years (1939-1945) spent first in Lushoto and then in Ngara and Biharamulo cannot have been easy. Except in special circumstances colonial administrators were asked to stay in their posts. Did Dad feel guilty not to be on active service? I know he and Mum worried a lot about the safety of their relatives as they intermittently got news of the situation in Britain. They knew that hundreds of citizens were being randomly killed and injured in German bombardments. There was a particularly terrible Blitz in May and June of 1941. They knew about the privations caused by food rationing, blackouts, fuel shortages and the like. They were concerned for the safety of Mum's brothers Denis and Leslie who had joined the army. They might even have taken some comfort from the fact that they too were suffering privations on account of the war. These included a freeze in salary and no home leave. Everyone was stretched and working overtime. Members of the administration had to be ever more resourceful with dwindling resources the bulk of which had to be diverted to the war effort. For instance, bully beef for the forces was in high demand so local chiefs were put under pressure to encourage their people to sell cattle. Raw materials like sisal and rubber had to be produced and then transported to the coast. The labour needed to achieve this was stretched to the limit because so many hundreds of Africans had been conscripted into the forces. Food was not rationed as it was in Britain and there was plenty of fruit and vegetables but staples like rice, wheat, bacon and ham were unobtainable. Mum used to boast that there was nothing she could not make out of bananas.

By the time Dad was posted to Mwanza on Lake Victoria in 1949 as District Commissioner, the years of stringency were over, the economy was moving and the administration was trying to make up for lost time. Sir Edward Twining was the newly appointed Governor of Tanganyika. He was a larger-than-life character, both physically and temperamentally and was exactly the sort of leader the colony needed after the bleak war years. His first task was to visit each of the eight provinces from his base in the capital to see what was going on for himself. As the Representative of the Crown he travelled in incredible style by road (in a Rolls Royce), by air, and by lake steamer. When he went by train he occupied special coaches which had been converted into bedrooms, a bath room, drawing room and dining room. His entourage consisted of the Provincial Commissioner of the Province in which he was travel-ling, his Private Secretary, the Public Relations Officer, an official photographer, his housekeeper and servants and members of a brass band.

He was very keen on the pageantry and show of imperial domin-ation and would don his white or navy blue ceremonial uniform and plumed hat for the huge *barazas* (public gatherings), tribal ceremonies, tattoos and fireworks that were organised for his enter-tainment. Between festivities and ceremonies he paid visits to the *boma,* the court house, the native treasury, the police station, the prison, and factories. Despite the frantic preparations beforehand, district officers, like my father, greatly appreciated the governor's attention; Twining was a pragmatic man who understood the frustrations and restrictions of their work, listened to their concerns and gave them practical support. He was an exacting taskmaster but was quick to give praise where praise was due. There is no doubt that he had a gift for getting the best out of people.

Twining's mission was to prepare Tanganyika for independence on a multi-racial basis. He believed that the economic strength that had to underpin independence could only be achieved by using the combined skills and resources of the Europeans, Asians and Africans. The timeline he considered necessary to achieve independence was at least 25 years. He set about breaking down existing social barriers by inviting people of all races to his official and private functions. A few old-timers in government considered him to be a dangerous radical but my parents approved of his policies and considered him a breath of fresh air. Twining's wife May always accompanied him on his travels. She dressed badly and was more reserved than her ebullient and charming husband but she was formidable in her own right. She had trained as a doctor and took a special interest in medical and social enterprises especially those

The Twinings with Princess Margaret

that helped African women and children. The Governor's conviction and enthusiasm brought new money, trade and industry into the country and with them came famous visitors like Prince Aly Khan and his beautiful wife Rita Hayworth. The Twinings had brought a touch of glamour to this most self-effacing of dependencies.

Being DC, Mwanza was a satisfying job. Dad arrived in time to help with the preparations for the Governor's visit at the end of July 1949; the two day whirlwind programme was deemed a success. My parents went to the dockside to wave goodbye as the Twining entourage embarked on the *S.S. Usoga* while the band played Auld Lang Syne. Now that the circus was over routine work could be resumed. There were so many jobs to be done and the DC's task was to make sure that they were completed by the various government departments and the District Officers for whom he was now responsible. Mwanza was growing rapidly and was the commercial centre for the densely populated Lake province. It was the terminus of the main railway, had a busy port and a new aerodrome. As well as the hospital it had a medical research unit. More resources were being put into education at every level. There was a large teachers' training centre at Pasiansi nearby and a big new prison was being constructed. The Geita gold mine to the west and Williamson's diamond mine to the south provided work for the locals and brought wealth to the whole country. The geologist Williamson, who had found the diamonds after years of fruitless excavating, and was said to be worth over £20 million was often away in Canada. My parents became friendly with the Indian manager Mr Chopra and his sophisticated wife. I can remember my parents coming back from one visit to the mine with an uncut ruby. It can't have been very valuable or my father would not have been allowed to accept it.

Under the influence of Sir Edward Twining Dad became persuaded that independence was coming sooner rather than later and that serious efforts must be made to help the country prepare for it. He had grown to have more respect for the African style of management though he always got cross when the motives and good intentions of the British administrators were misconstrued or impugned. He never doubted that whatever he and his colleagues did, they did in the best interests of the Africans and the wellbeing of the country. In 1948 he contributed a revealing article entitled *Mens Sana* in the publication *Tanganyika Notes and Records*. He points out that a questioning minority of the population is growing more mistrustful of colonial government and more unrealistic in their demands. He suggests that this problem should be countered by propaganda: "Propaganda in the good sense, meaning the dissemination of truth and knowledge on those subjects about which misunderstanding has arisen." He wants Africans to have a better understanding of what the government is trying to do. He recommends the creation of a Public Relations department with an appropriate budget.

Perhaps this very article had something to do with the fact that at the end of 1955 Dad himself was appointed Director of an enlarged and active Public Relations Department in Dar es Salaam. At this stage, considering the political climate (with increasing pressure from the Africans for independence) this job was a very important and sensitive one. He had a staff of some 13 Europeans, 16 Asians and 180 Africans. All the official photographs were taken by a brilliant photographer called John Mitchell-Hedges who was supported by a handsome turbaned Sikh called Mohinder Singh. Alan Neville, the chief press officer was an experienced journalist who had worked for the *East African Standard* in Nairobi. The department was housed in a cluster of ramshackle wooden huts north of the main Secretariat. These had been erected as temporary buildings during the war but appeared to have become permanent fixtures.

My father faced two main challenges in his two years as Director of Public Relations for which he received a salary of £2,500. The first was to reach out to the African population; the voice of the nationalists under the leadership of Julius Nyerere was becoming more strident; TANU (the Tanganyika African National Union party) founded in 1954 was calling for "Africa for the Africans" and "One Man One Vote." The slogan on its banner was *Uhuru* – a swahili word derived from Arabic meaning the liberty of an emancipated slave. Julius Nyerere was rather an unlikely nationalist leader. He was the son of a chief of the Zanaki tribe from Butiama in the Musoma district of Lake Province. He had been educated in a Catholic mission where his brilliance and talents had been recognised and nurtured. He received scholarships to go to Makerere College in Uganda and then to Edinburgh University. He became involved in active politics when he was a thirty-three year old teacher at a secondary school run by the White Fathers. He was modest, softly-spoken and disinterested in acquiring wealth. He was also a resolute and inspirational leader with a gift for oratory.

At first Nyerere agreed with Twining that the Africans would not be ready for independence for a long time, but, by the time my father arrived in Dar, Nyerere was lobbying the United Nations and London for independence within a decade. Although Twining, who had always underrated Nyerere, was dragging his feet, the writing was on the wall for all to see. My father and his colleagues knew that an accelerated effort had to be made to educate, inform and train Africans for the task of governing themselves. This was a challenging shift in emphasis from occasions like the annual visit by a Royal Navy warship or the opening of Legislative Council which hitherto had occupied the department. New energy and resources were directed to the Swahili press and radio which were obviously going to be vital in the dissemination of information to the African population.

The government press printed a daily news sheet in Swahili called *Mwangaza*, a weekly newssheet called *Habri za Leo* and a monthly magazine called *Mambo Leo* which had a huge circulation. Numerous cyclostyled newspapers were published and distributed in English and Swahili to the districts. News bulletins were supplied to the broadcasting stations. The Public Relations department produced the official Gazette, notices, circulars and reports. The editor-in-chief of the Swahili newspapers was a talented and liberal-minded Irishman called Randal Sadleir who believed unreservedly in Africa for the Africans. He was socially unconventional and got to know Africans on a genuine basis of equality. He would invite talented young Africans to his home for regular discussions and he drank with them in the Cosy Café. He did this at a time when the Dar es Salaam Club, the Gymkhana and Golf clubs were still open to whites only. Legislative Council meetings had only recently provided simultaneous translation from English to Swahili. In his book *Tanzania: Journey to Republic* Sadleir admitted that "Some of my senior colleagues had an aversion to educated Africans, particularly those from Christian missions whom they thought less honest than Muslims and too big for their boots. They also quite sincerely felt that to socialise with locals after working with them all day put too much of a strain on their wives and families." My parents were much more open-minded than these types, but they were not as pro-active as Randal Sadleir, a genuine friend of Julius

Nyerere who invited him to stay on after independence. Sadleir describes my father as "a tall, dark, handsome man with a shy smile and a twinkle in his eye. He was quiet, serious and conscientious. As the quintessentially English grandson of the late Victorian poet laureate Austin Dobson, one could never have imagined him doing anything mean or dishonourable. He gave me a warm welcome, though he regarded me as impulsively Irish and felt it his duty to 'rein me in' from time to time when excessive enthusiasm got the better of me. He and his brilliant wife Barbara remained good friends for many years."

The other challenge which was Princess Margaret's visit in 1956 seems much more frivolous but was nevertheless taken very seriously at the time. Being a traditionalist and staunch monarchist Sir Edward Twining was determined to make the most of it. He wanted to turn the visit into a multi-racial celebration of Empire and a stimulus for loyalty to the Crown despite the rumblings in the background. Elaborate preparations were started six months ahead of time. These included the addition of a new wing for Government House. Typically this building project turned out to be a nightmare. In the end the last workman left in the afternoon before the royal party arrived. Routes, transport, accommodation, travel and celebratory events all had to be arranged. Twining left nothing to chance and insisted on being present at rehearsals all over the territory. The Princess arrived in the royal yacht *Britannia* on 8th October with 1.5 tons of baggage, an entourage of twelve and with 55 journalists in tow. She was obliged to open a new dock before being driven in procession to Government House past crowds of adults and children waving Union flags. That evening there was a state banquet. Despite a punishing schedule Princess Margaret behaved impeccably and even seemed to enjoy herself. During her tour of the country she travelled 1700 miles and shook hands with over a thousand people. She inspected the Girl Guides, Boy Scouts, an experimental sisal factory, a game reserve, hospitals and schools. She attended numerous dinners, tattoos and *ngomas*.

During this memorable "Year of the Princess" Dad was responsible for the activities of the local and foreign media and worked relentlessly hard. The stress brought on recurring back problems and his desire to retire. He was often in agony and took to working standing up at a raised desk. Thankfully the visit was deemed a great success and he and his department received their fair share of the praise. But the visit did nothing to stem the surge towards independence. Twining left the colony a year later. His popularity amongst all races was acknowledged but he was criticized for being paternalistic. His successor, Sir Richard Turnbull, had none of Twining's misgivings about the speed of change and made it his business to drive independence through. This came in 1961. That it took place without violence, bitterness or fighting was largely due to the sagacity and skill of Julius Nyerere who became the young nation's first President.

Chapter 7

DO as Novelist

I wish I had asked Dad which posting had been his favourite. They were all so different perhaps he would have found it difficult to say. Isolated posts had many disadvantages but the freedom to act without interference and the scope for responsibility must have been heady stuff. On the other hand, the larger stations offered more variety and opportunity for a social life. Sadly, Dad did not keep a record or diary of his working life and any letters he wrote have disappeared. But I can safely make some inferences about his experiences from the four novels he wrote during his time in Tanganyika. The books also show how his attitudes as a colonial administrator and his relationship with the people he governed changed with the passage of time. He starts each book with the same disclaimer: "The characters, the Protectorate and the places mentioned in this book as being in East Africa, the situations and the events, are entirely fictitious." Yet the township Dena could be a prototype for any medium-sized town in Tanganyika. The complicated and intimate relationships would have been only too familiar in a small tightly knit ex-pat community. The plots and dramas which centred round conflicts with the native population were based on experience but most intriguing of all is the change in the balance of power between the rulers and the ruled which is charted through all four books and obviously reflected Dad's own changing attitude to race relations and colonial rule.

While he was alive I failed to give my father sufficient credit for his writing. I know that my own children have taken my published works very much for granted and take no trouble to re-read them. I was just the same with my father: a prophet in his own country and all that. Now that I have perused Dad's novels afresh and with greater attention I think they are rather good. There were many non-fiction books and pamphlets written about colonial life in

Tanganyika. I have also unearthed a few delightful memoirs, but, to my knowledge, my father was the only district officer in Tanganyika who attempted to fictionalise his experiences. The Tanganyika railway inspired his first book entitled *Mail Train* which was written during the war and published by Hodder and Stoughton in 1946. It is a detective story cum thriller set on a train journey from Dar to Mwanza. During the journey there is a hoax, burglaries, two hold-ups and a botched attempt at murder. The characters come straight out of a game of *Cluedo:* Mr Smythe, Mrs Accrington, Professor and Mrs Derwent and bossy Mrs Boothby. The heroes are the hard-bitten District Commissioner and his bull terrier Daisy. The attractive Miss French provides a romantic angle, Mr Black is the train inspector and the engine driver is a Scot. This train could have been the overnight train from London to Edinburgh or Agatha Christie's *Orient Express.* The African passengers confined to 3rd class, and the Indians to 2nd class do not have a role to play. The populace is referred to in asides like "the smell of hot perspiring humanity." The attitude of my father, who was considered to be a hard-working, dedicated and able administrator was typical of most Europeans in this era. Africans were there to serve and do menial tasks. They were not the social equals of the Europeans. They were not even significant enough to be the villains in my father's novel. The thing I like best about this book is the dedication: "To my three small daughters, in spite of whose help this book has been completed."

By the time he got down to writing *The Inescapable Wilderness* published in 1952, Dad had developed immeasurably as a writer and observer. The blurb describes the novel as giving "a vivid picture of the difficulties of East African town life as it is to-day – the conflict between the old and the new, the stresses and strains of racial relationships, the aspirations of the black man and the problems which they create for the white." The main character is an unmarried Provincial Commissioner called Richard Winter who is faced with politically motivated strikes and riots by Africans who are protesting against a scheme to move them from their land to create a commercial sunflower project. This scenario may well have been a veiled reference to the government's disastrous groundnut scheme where huge amounts of money had been spent on an unsuccessful attempt to grow groundnuts in an unsuitable area. The tense situation in Dena has an effect on the relationships of the members of the small white community. Despite the heavy demands on him, Winter finds time to have an affair with the wife of one of his administrative officers. On the other hand, he redeems himself by also finding time to pay regular visits to his faithful African servant of eighteen years who is dying of TB in the local hospital.

The PC is an ambitious, chilly character who is not popular with his subordinates. But he works extremely hard, knows his job and gets the upper hand at the end of the day when the malefactors are rounded up and put into jail. He has an interesting relationship with James Forrest, a DC in an outlying district. Unusually, this DC has been left in the same place for eight years which is the way he likes it. He is not interested in promotion, hates interference from his superiors and knows his district inside and out and from top to bottom. Forrest thinks of the natives he governs in the following way. "He wanted to be their father; in a way – though it sounded ridiculously sentimental – he loved them; just as he loved their intractable country and the beauty of the wild flowers that softened its fierceness." During the riot the PC is not able to contact his subordinate and so has to trust that he can manage the situation in his area without assistance. Needless to say, DC Forrest acquits himself with skill and courage because he is ultimately trusted and liked by the people he governs.

The hero of *District Commissioner* published in 1954 is John Fenton whose character is very different from the flamboyant

A Shauri

Redmayne from whom he takes over. He too is faced with restive Africans egged on by political agitators. They are protesting at having to cull their cattle on government orders as a measure to prevent soil erosion. Here is a DC who is quiet, sensible and dedicated to his job. Race relations have moved on apace. The town council has African and Indian members who are invited to drinks parties by the DC's wife. Mr Khimji an Asian trader on the council is a very sympathetic character. One of the black councillors dares to address the DC in the following terms: "I cannot conceal that Africans have much suspicion of the government. Everywhere they have seen Europeans taking the land of Africans, and they see clearly that the Europeans do not wish to allow them to take part in the affairs of the government, making excuses that Africans are not properly educated. But if Africans are not educated is it not the fault of the Europeans who have kept education from us, so that we shall remain in servitude?" In my father's last novel, *Colour Blind,* the African comes of age. A young black graduate from an English university who has a responsible government post falls in love with an English teacher. The affair ends badly, but in the end it is the Europeans who retreat, while Joshua Semikula becomes the radical leader of an independence movement.

Many of these themes resonate with what I know of my father's working life. He (like Winter) had one faithful servant who stayed with him for all but the last three years in Africa. He felt great loyalty, affection and gratitude for this man who was called Issa Ngosingosi. Issa could be quarrelsome with the other servants and frequently had *shauris* with his wives, but his qualities and abilities greatly outweighed his few shortcomings. He could read, write and was highly intelligent. He was a creative cook, a very good mechanic and a competent handyman. In fact he could do just about everything. He was an indispensable person to have on safari or on long journeys when the car would inevitably break down along the way. He was able to mend the carburettor, change the fan belt and patch the tires. On one occasion my father had to rush him to hospital when he swallowed petrol while trying to unblock an air lock. My parents did not just rely on him for practicalities but for the wisdom and knowledge of his own country that he shared with them. Dad gave him a gift of money when he left Africa. Issa spent this well and wisely on the education of his sons who kept my

parents informed of their progress over the years through a series of delightful letters written in English. Two of them came to England to study and visited us in our home in Kent. They ended up with professional government jobs and were able to afford the dowries to get married.

Issa retired to Biharamulo where he lived to a ripe old age, outliving both my parents. He wrote regular letters in Swahili to my parents for many years. We were told that he kept photos of our family on the walls of his house. We too have photos of him and a portrait which hangs in Harriet's kitchen. When my father died in 1981 my mother received a touching letter from Issa's oldest son Ramadhani. In it he wrote, "I am deeply sorry to learn about the death of my beloved father the late Mr Dobson. I do not find the right words to express my sorrows. I have been robbed of my life pride. All the successes and our worldly fortunes (I mean our family) – depended to a greater extent on the foresight of the Dobsons. We all were educated under the good guidance of Mr Dobson, our houses came to us through the wise guidance of the Dobsons and what is more, unlike other ex overseas servicemen the Dobsons kept continuous contacts even after more than 20 years of departure."

Another fictional theme which rings true to real life is the weight of responsibility carried by often very young colonial administrators. The heroes of the books are always DCs who are dedicated and hard working to a fault. They have to deal with dramas and take decisions on their own, knowing that if these decisions turn out to be wrong they will be carpeted by their Provincial Commissioner. My father was a conscientious person and tended to worry. When he was a DO he was ticked off by one of his superiors for not putting in enough social appearances at the club. When I was old enough to understand something of his working life, I was struck by the numbers of files that were always piled up on his desk. These were made of thick brown paper and the thin typed papers interlaced with carbon sheets were secured inside the covers with a piece of green string with metal tags on the end. He kept a stick of red sealing wax on his desk which he used for confidential mail. He would melt it with a match onto the back of the envelope and then press his signet ring down on top. He wore this ring embossed with crossed bear paws on the little finger of his left hand. He gave each of us girls a similar signet ring when we reached the age of twenty-one.

In his delightful memoir, *A Fanfare of Trumpets* John Lewis-Barned graphically describes the burden common to all administrators. "There was a great deal of administrative paperwork at Utete so that desks groaned with the weight of files which dutiful messengers brought in until the piles were sometimes so high that they fell in a heap on the floor to be carried away again. In fact Ursula (his wife) helped me in the office as there was a shortage of African staff and a mass of work to do. As usual I seem to have taken on Sub-Accountancy, Local Authority Treasury and Finance generally, as well as Ploughing Scheme Accounts, Police, (all eight of them), Prisons and Land and Economics, which meant price control of sugar, flour and rice." I know that my mother's presence in Dad's life would have greatly alleviated the burden he carried. Not only was she wise and intelligent enough to share his worries but she did a lot of secretarial work for him.

In his novels Dad highlights the crucial nature of the relationship between a DO and his superior officer. He had good relationships with his DCs and PCs as far as I know but there were people in the service who were not so lucky. I remember my parents talking about colleagues under intolerable strain who had fallen ill, become alcoholics, suffered nervous breakdowns or even committed suicide. The long hours and absences could be hard on wives too. The novels are full of emotional intrigue and even extra-marital affairs which certainly reflected real life situations amongst the ex-pat community. I like to think that my parents did not stray. They seemed to get on so well and were able to support each other in difficult times. They also both appreciated the opportunities and excitement of Dad's career in Africa.

The development of Dad's political views can be clearly charted through the novels. In the 30s and 40s he had a benevolent but patronising view of Africans whom he considered to be like children who, as yet, could not manage their own affairs. There is a telling episode in *The Inescapable Wilderness* when the nursing sister reflects on one of her black patients. "He would be dead in a week. No one would grieve for long, she imagined; Africans forget quickly. His wife and relatives would take a holiday and wail for three days; the shillings he had buried in his hut would be dug up and divided out; then he would fade from the mind of the living. How simple to be able to dispose of life, of dreams, of memories in three days." In another passage, an old-timer comforts an idealistic newcomer after he has hit an African rioter over the head. "It's all right. He'll come round in a minute. Their skulls are like bits of wood." Was my father unconscious of the racial prejudice and ignorance embedded in these descriptions or was he putting these words into the mouths of fictionalised characters who he considered crass?

In the 1960s many former colonies achieved independence and the British Empire transmogrified into the Commonwealth. The Empire was stripped of its glamour by revisionist historians. Colonialism was criticised and demeaned. In multi-cultural Britain the derring-do adventure stories of Empire builders, white hunters, and the military were expunged from history books, posters, advertisements and comic strips. It became unfashionable to be proud of our colonial history. My poor parents must have suffered from the strident opinions I formed at Oxford University. Instead of being interested in their working lives I priggishly lectured them about the iniquities of colonial rule. I agreed with the author Joanna Lewis who described the British Empire as "nasty, brutish and in shorts." My views must have been painful for my parents, who remained remarkably patient with me.

I now wish to record my revised assessment. Colonial rule was short – less than fifty years in the case of Tanganyika. It was largely conducted in shorts but it was not brutish. The people of Tanganyika did not invite the British to be their rulers. We imposed ourselves upon them, thereby committing an arrogant injustice which changed their history and cultural identity for ever. But if one puts this fundamental premise to one side and accepts colonial rule as a given, then I think that public servants like my father worked hard and honestly to deliver as much security, peace, justice, education, health and improved agriculture as finance and time allowed them. I am no longer ashamed of the role my parents played and I can look back on my childhood with wonder and curiosity less trammelled by guilt. And too late, alas, I can say that I am proud of my father as administrator and novelist.

Chapter 8

Mum's Work

In: *I Remember It Well* a book of personal reminiscences by colonialists, Jane Shadbolt wrote, "It was taken for granted that one would be a splendid little woman, bravely coping with hardship and isolation, always ready with hospitality for all-comers and bearing and raising children with the minimum of fuss and inconvenience to one's husband." Mum was such a splendid little woman though there was no doubt that she and my father were equals. She took to life in Africa with relish. Some spouses took to drink, had affairs or returned to Britain separately. But from the beginning Mum energetically and positively involved herself in everything. She realized that Swahili was indispensable and set about learning it as quickly as possible. As Dad had to have lessons to pass the formal exams required by government, he helped her acquire a good standard. Mum always detested housework and was glad to have servants to do it for her, but she needed to learn all the household skills necessary to train them. Until our Mwanza days, domestic conditions were pretty basic. German-built houses were considered the most desirable properties. They were made of brick with thick walls and deep verandas. Otherwise, the houses occupied by British government officials were standard: the exterior walls were white-washed, the roof was made of grey corrugated iron which got very hot in the dry season and clattered when the rains fell, windows and doors had panels of wire netting to let fresh air in and to keep mosquitoes and insects out. There were two to three bedrooms, a sitting-room, dining-room, a bathroom and a veranda. The kitchen was a separate building outside, as was the *choo* (a long-drop lavatory) which was a wooden box over a deep hole. The Public Works Department (PWD) provided standardised furniture which was instantly recognisable. The entitlement was: 2 khaki coloured armchairs and a sofa, a bookcase, a desk, a dining table and 6-8 chairs, a glass-fronted sideboard, beds, and bedside tables. There were usually built-in wardrobes. Cutlery, kitchen utensils and linen were not provided.

For years we lived without mainline electricity or hot running water. A portable fridge was an essential item and was run off paraffin. Hospitals, offices and some grand houses had noisy and notoriously unreliable generators to provide light and heat, but most Europeans used hurricane Dietz or pressure lamps at night. Dad used to trim the wicks and replenish the methylated spirit. I can recall with nostalgia the sound of hissing, the smell of spirit and the light brightening as Dad worked the plunger. The light from the lamps attracted moths and insects that would ping against the glass shade when they collided with it. Flies and insects came with the territory. We called them *dudus*. For anti-insect protection the bed legs stood in tins of paraffin and mosquito nets were hung from the ceiling. Poisonous spiders and scorpions were a real hazard. Shaking out shoes, cushions and canvas chairs became an ingrained habit. Once when we were visiting Ukerewe Island, Dad was stung by a scorpion which was concealed in the fold of a deckchair and had to be rushed to the nearest dispensary. At dusk a servant would walk through the rooms with a DDT flit. The use of this powerful chlorinated insecticide is prohibited now, but it was used liberally in our day to keep down mosquitoes. The smell was unpleasant but it does not appear to have done us any harm.

Water for the bath and basins was heated outside in *debbies* on a wood fire. In its functional simplicity the *debby* was one of the most valuable objects in use at this epoch. It was a four gallon paraffin tin. Once emptied of its contents, and with the lid cut off, and wooden handles inserted, the *debby* had multiple uses. Water was heated in an outside boiler on a wood or charcoal fire and then transported to the bath. In the dry season when water was scarce, *debbies* were refilled with the dirty bath water and poured over the garden plants. Another water-saving device was to scrub the dirty pots and pans with sand or earth before rinsing them in water. Drinking water had to be boiled. Because water was such a precious commodity in the dry season, we were taught not to waste it. When the rains did come between March and May, and again in November and December, water was collected and stored in a large exterior barrel or metal container. Bath water was scanty and had to be shared. To this day the sound of carelessly running tap water makes me feel anxious.

The first task Mum set herself was to make her PWD dwelling look less standardised. She managed to do this despite the fact that until the war she had to move every two years. Mum's personal touches included English prints on the wall, books (albeit infested with cockroaches and stained with mildew) on the bookshelves and cut flowers in vases. These were also important symbols of home and civilization. The car, the piano, the gramophone, and the cutlery canteen were the only substantial possessions my parents privately owned. When Mum decided she needed some pretty curtains, cushions and bedspreads she bought a second-hand Singer sewing machine and taught herself to sew. She became so attached to this machine that she brought it back to England with her when she left Africa. She worked a treadle plate with her feet and turned a handle with her right hand while feeding in fabric with her left hand.

She made clothes for us and dresses for herself. If she couldn't find the fabric she needed in the Indian *dukas* she got it sent out from England together with paper patterns. Mum was not a patient person and used to rush at her sewing with the result that sleeves were put in the wrong way round and mistakes were made. She either unpicked the stitching with loud complaints or said, "Dash it! I'm going to leave it as it is. A man on a galloping horse won't notice." For years she dressed the three of us in identical clothes. It was probably less trouble. As I look at the old photographs of our childhood I think she did rather a good job. At the time I think we were not displeased either, except on one occasion when she made us sundresses out of a hideous green black and yellow fabric. One of the few times I saw my mother cry was when Pedro the *dhobi* ruined a nylon party dress she had made for one of us by using the charcoal iron on it. I remember being very shocked by this. She cheered me up by saying, " Don't worry. I'll get over it. What's a silly pink party dress in the grand scheme of things?"

Mum got more pleasure creating a garden and a vegetable patch than she did from the house. Gardening was a therapeutic occupation for her. She would get seeds sent out from England, cuttings from neighbours and seedlings from the agricultural stations. She would have a garden boy to help her but liked to get her own hands dirty. What with poor earth, alternating droughts and heavy rains, locusts and hungry wild animals, she was perpetually locked in a grim battle with nature. Sometimes she won and sometimes nature

Mum in her garden

won. But if anyone could cultivate cannas, marigolds, nasturtiums, petunias and geraniums it would have been my mother. The heavily scented frangipani and the vivid bougainvillea were staples in most European gardens. The Germans had been keen on growing trees and our homes generally had mature nandi flame, jacaranda, wattle, mango and guava trees. The vegetable garden required more work and constant weeding but provided us with lettuces, tomatoes, potatoes, maize, cabbages and pumpkins.

Cooking was another skill my mother had to learn fast. *Mrs Beeton's Book of Household Management,* which she took out to Africa, proved of little use. A PWD house in the African outback had nothing in common with a Victorian household run on principles of cleanliness, order, punctuality and method by a team of servants. The detached kitchen was an unhygienic smoky annexe equipped with a wood burning Dover stove, pots and pans and pyrex dishes. African servants had many virtues but order, punctuality and method were not among them. Mum absorbed some basic cooking steps from the recipes and then she and Issa experimented with the limited ingredients they could lay their hands on. Between them, they learnt how to do wonders with scrawny chickens, bananas, pawpaws, mangoes, dried custard, eggs and condensed milk. Over the years she compiled her own book of recipes which she picked up from other households. From my mother I learnt to make delicious stews out of the most unpromising ingredients, and I still use her African recipe for cold chicken curry.

Entertaining was the glue that kept the ex-patriot community cohesive and in good heart and the club provided a common venue for social and sporting activities. In isolated settlements, the

Europeans would meet for sundowners (drinks) and meals at the club or in each other's houses where they played bridge. There was always a round of parties at Christmas and New Year which swept up anyone living alone. If a new government official and family arrived, a senior officer would put them up until they were settled. Anyone travelling through could expect to be housed and fed by a fellow European. We frequently had visitors to stay, and on a few occasions some of these outstayed their welcome.

Administrators like my father were at the top of the pecking order, while those engaged in agriculture, mines, public health, prisons, police and railways had lower status in a subtle way. Mum was socially self-confident enough not to feel the need to be snobbish. Within the parameters of small-town mentality she tried to be as unconventional as possible. She was a good bridge player, had a penchant for word games and earned a reputation for giving lively parties.

Formal visits by the Provincial Commissioner, sometimes with a VIP from Britain in tow, could be alarming. Dad would try and make sure that the office was running smoothly while Mum would pray that the chickens would not disappear before they were killed for the table. They managed to avoid causing offence to their superiors and Dad's climb up the ladder of promotion proceeded without a hitch. Edward Lumley who wrote an interesting little book called: *Forgotten Mandate,* about his life as a district officer in Tanganyika did cross his superiors on a number of occasions and his career suffered for it. A brilliant and principled Irish man he was not afraid of taking risks and acting on his own initiative with the unintended result that he was sent to a hardship post and his promotion was stalled.

As wife of the District Commissioner, and subsequently Deputy Provincial Commissioner in Mwanza, Mum was faced with increased social obligations. Some wives might have found this rather daunting but she seized the opportunity for meeting the most entertaining and interesting people around. St George's Day, Armistice Day and the Queen's birthday were annual fixtures in every posting. They were marked by parades and formal dinners which were larded with toasts and patriotic speeches. We loved seeing Dad in full dress uniform or in a dinner jacket and Mum (always the belle-of-the-ball) in a long halter-neck frock.

In addition to her domestic tasks, Mum worked part-time. In the early days she gave Dad secretarial and clerical assistance and accompanied him on safari. The first record I have of her doing official work is in 1940 in Lushoto which had been built as a hill station for the German government. They both loved living and working in this little town on the edge of the Usambara mountain range which is part of the ancient Eastern Arc. Every little knoll and spur on the flanks of the valleys had a cluster of two or three huts and a cattle pen. These looked picturesque and were connected with each other by narrow winding paths. The Usambara area has a very special ecology which harbours unusual plants and animals that are found nowhere else on earth. All this would have fascinated Mum and the forest and lush woodland would have been refreshing after the hot bushland of Maswa. Best of all she could keep horses and go riding again. Lushoto had such a pleasant climate and situation that the Governor followed the German example and picked it as a retreat. Governor's Lodge built in 1937 resembled a Dutch Colonial house and was surrounded by a lovely garden with running water, English flowers and peach and pear trees. The Governor, his aides and friends used the house in the hottest months between December and April. Their seasonal presence greatly enlivened social life for the Europeans.

I don't know whether Mum had a paid administrative post in the *boma* at Lushoto, or whether she was commissioned to undertake specific tasks for local government, but I do know that she undertook a detailed study of the Wasambaa people. She wrote up the findings of this study in a long and erudite article which was published in *Tanganyika Notes and Records* in 1940. Her brief was to collate the native rights and laws of land tenure observed by the Wasambaa who farmed the plains below the Wasambara scarp. To do this she spent days and days talking to the sub-chiefs and elders from the various sub-chiefdoms of the district as well as to the occupiers of the land and their wives. Information was also obtained from Pastor Gleiss and Pastor Wohlrab of the German Bethel Mission who had lived for over thirty years among the Wasambaa.

A particular native area was chosen for a detailed survey: With the help of the local elders who knew the boundaries and history of every field, comprehensive maps were made, the accuracy of which was vouched for by my mother who personally measured and marked every field on the map. The article describes the situation on the land and concludes with a number of recommendations to deal with potential problems in the future such as inevitable land erosion. This research project, which so impressed me with its depth and knowledge made sense of a story I was recently told by John Lewis-Barned. The story has it that an official was visiting my father's station and asked for some information on Native Affairs. "Don't ask me about that" replied my father. "You need to talk to Bib. She's the expert in this area." I'm sure she was. Her knowledge of the customs and ways of some African tribes would have expanded through the work she did for Hans Cory when we moved to Mwanza and she became his assistant.

Hans Cory was an anthropologist in the service of the government. He is one of the characters I remember best from my childhood. He and his wife Lily were Viennese. They were both very short. Hans was plump and Lily was tiny and delicate with mournful deep-set eyes. As children we were fascinated by their distinctive foreignness and strange accents. Lily was an artist who painted in oils. The only painting of hers we acquired was the portrait of Issa. Hans Cory was basically a self-taught anthropologist and ethnologist. He had grown up in a musical family in Vienna. As a young man he had developed an interest in African song, dance and Swahili poetry which had brought him out to Tanganyika where he settled down. Here he set about learning all he could about the rites, ceremonies, secret societies and plant medicine of the Sukumu, Hay, Zinza and Kerewe tribes who lived around Biharamulo and Lake Victoria. He advised the administration on native affairs in general and was brought in to investigate specific problems ranging from murders, venereal disease and cattle theft to witchcraft.

I did not know at the time that Hans Cory was born Hans Koritschoner and came to Tanganyika during German rule. He fought and was wounded while fighting with the German army under Von Lettow-Vorbeck. Ernest Hemingway met him on the hunting trip for the elusive kudu which he wrote up in *Green Hills of Africa*. His meeting with Kandisky (Hans Koritschoner) obviously delighted him. "To run into one (a white man) on this road where you met only an occasional Indian trader and the steady migration of the natives out of the famine country, to have him look like a caricature of Benchley in Tyrolean costume, to have him know your name, to call you a poet, to have read the *Querschnitt*, to be an admirer of Joachim Ringelnatz and to want to talk about Rilke, was too fantastic to deal with." By the time we knew Hans his German surname name had been dropped and he was working for the British.

He had amassed a unique collection of hundreds of clay figurines which were housed in a German tower in his Mwanza garden. This also doubled up as the office where Mum worked. These little figures were displayed on shelves. Amazingly, we young-sters were allowed to go into this tower room on our own

sometimes. The majority of figures were male and many of these had pronounced phallic erections. We took a salacious interest in the rude ones which always sent us into paroxysms of mirth. What a pity that we were not mature enough to appreciate what we were seeing: the rites involving these figurines were so secret that the very act of having acquired so many was in itself interesting. Some figurines would have been used in the circumcision rites for boys and girls reaching puberty. Others would have been used for the passing on of sage advice. For instance, the figure of a hare was accompanied by the following axiom, "The hare is cleverer than most animals, but he is never anxious to start a fight." An amusing figure of a man holding field glasses carried a warning to beware of whites with the words, "The Europeans can see beyond the range of other people." In the acknowledgements in the preface of his illustrated book, entitled, *African Figurines* dated 1956, Hans Cory wrote, "I have pleasure in thanking my secretary, Mrs E.B. Dobson for her never-ceasing interest and assistance in the preparation of this work."

Mum was also involved in many of the voluntary associations that were active in the colony as well as in every corner of the Empire. She joined the Women's Service League which brought women of all races together through good works like the running of children's clinics, the distribution of library books and social activities. She took a leading role in the Girl Guide movement which was particularly popular with the Asian community. There is a photo of her taking a salute from the Mwanza company during a ceremonial parade. She is wearing a navy-blue uniform and beret and looks really smart.

Mum would urge us to join in her guiding activities during the holidays. But I am afraid I was snobbish and uncooperative. I thought tying knots, making campfires and painting pictures were occupations beneath contempt. I was faintly put off by the military overtones – the uniforms, the marching and the swearing of allegiance to God, King and Country. Many of the worthy movements like the Salvation Army, the Boys Brigades and the Boy Scout movement founded at the height of Empire had similar military overtones of rank and discipline. Undoubtedly we missed out on a lot, including the chance to socialise with Asian and African children. Mum took us to tea parties with her Indian women friends but we were not enamoured of these either because of the fizzy drinks and sugary cakes we were obliged to consume.

Mum did part-time work for the secretariat during their last posting in Dar. I later heard, quite by chance, that she worked in the department which dealt with sorcery and witchcraft. Even

Muslim or Christian Africans tended to retain a belief in animism and the power of witchdoctors. It was very important to understand the power these beliefs could exert. Even employees working in the *boma* would suddenly disappear or refuse to do something on account of a superstition. Since natives tended to ascribe illness or bad fortune to the work of evil spells, they turned to witchdoctors to remove these curses. There were white witches who practised the benign arts of healing and spiritualism. Many a rational district officer has told tales of Africans getting better after the ministrations of a white witch. Sometimes a local witchdoctor wielded more influence than a chief and it proved expedient to work with him. Other witchdoctors however, practised black arts which involved human body parts and the casting of evil spells. District officers would try and bring such practitioners to justice if murder or kidnap was involved. In August 1956 during our last summer holiday in Africa a famous and charismatic healer witchdoctor called Nguvumali set up camp on the outskirts of Dar. Thousands of Africans flocked to his meetings every day. Many of them paid him to have evil spells removed. Undoubtedly there would have been policemen present to keep an eye on proceedings but there was no question of closing down such a popular gathering.

During our last two years in Africa Mum had fewer official duties but continued to entertain friends and the children of friends with her usual brio and originality. A second cousin of my mother recently told me of the welcome she had received from my parents: Ursula and John Lewis-Barned came out to Tanganyika in 1956, some years later John fell ill and was transferred to a hospital in Dodoma, this is what Ursula told me. "I arrived in Dar with a turkey and a badly behaved dog just in time for Christmas. Your parents took me in and looked after me for months until John was able to leave hospital. They were incredibly kind and neither of us has forgotten it."

Chapter 9

Childhood

My older sister Harriet was born on 21st January 1940 while my parents were posted to Lushoto. Her delivery took place in the European hospital in Tanga which was the second largest town in the territory. Eighteen months later, on the 23rd September 1941, I was born in the same hospital. According to family mythology my birth was attended by a gory accident. Mum would tell me the story as an explanation for my sticking-out belly button which was more like that of an African *toto* and quite different to those of my sisters. Apparently, after I had been born and the umbilical cord cut and tied, I was removed from my mother and taken to another room in the hospital. Mum, who was supposed to be resting was overcome by a presentiment that something was wrong with me. She put on her dressing gown and shuffled down the corridor to investigate. She found me lying in a pool of blood in my cot. The doctor had made a botch of tying the umbilical cord which had to be remedied. This tale of being saved from drowning in my own blood "in the nick of time" made me feel very special – just like the *Thirteenth Orphan* which was a favourite childhood book. The thirteenth orphan had a birthmark which meant that she was lucky and no harm would come to her in the end though she was treated abominably in the meantime.

It wasn't until I gave birth to my first son in the comfort and safety of a large London NHS hospital that I began to have an inkling of my mother's experience of childbirth. She certainly would not have had regular checks, ultrasounds or blood tests during her pregnancies. She travelled from Lushoto to Tanga (a distance of 109 miles) to stay with friends before her due date so that she could give birth under the care of a white doctor in a proper hospital. My father was never with her during childbirth. By the time my younger sister Janet (commonly known as Jane) came along my parents had moved yet again, this time to an isolated station called Biharamulo which lay to the far west near the Belgian Congo border. Jane was born on 5th July 1942 in a missionary hospital in Burundi. My mother's story about Jane's birth centred on the rather fierce nun in charge at the mission hospital. When my mother complained at having to use the outside long-drop lavatory during labour she was sharply told, "you are in charge of your own body and can make it do what you want." It was fortunate that my sister was not born headfirst in the *choo* hole.

Our upbringing was a strange mix of African and English cultures with the latter predominating. When we were young we were unaware of any dichotomy in this. Africans carry their babies strapped to their backs in colourful cloths until they are big enough to walk. Perhaps this is why, unless they are starving, they seldom cry. The babies are breast fed until the milk dries up. They play as toddlers at the feet of their mother as she sweeps the mud floor of the hut, washes clothes in the river, pounds cassavas or cooks *posho* and stews which are eaten by hand. By the age of seven or eight they are considered old enough to do chores or herd cattle.

From the moment we were born we were initiated into English ways. For our christenings we wore, in turn, my father's long white embroidered muslin robe. We were dressed in little white dresses and bonnets. We were put down to sleep in a cot (albeit draped in a mosquito net) and were wheeled around in a Silver Cross pram. This equipment would have been passed onto us second-hand. My mother sang us all the traditional nursery rhymes like *Ring-a-Ring of Roses, The Grand Old Duke of York, London Bridge is Falling Down, Oranges and Lemons, Baa Baa Blacksheep* and *I Had a Little Nut Tree*. Now in my turn I am singing these to my grand children. With the use of English textbooks and correspondence courses my mother taught us how to read, write and do basic arithmetic We learnt to read from the *Janet and John* readers and progressed to Enid Blyton's *Noddy* books. We had a chart of the Kings and Queens of England which we learnt by heart. We looked at illustrations of snow scenes, ice skating, country cottages and townscapes with rows of red brick houses with tiled roofs. Later when we could read by ourselves we became immersed in Arthur Ransome's *Swallows and Amazons* and Enid Blyton's *Secret Seven* and *Famous Five* adventure series. There was something fantastical about these stories and settings which would have been so mundane to our compatriots in England. But, I now see we were the poorer for not tapping into the rich source of oral story-telling which was right on our doorstep.

Every tribe in East Africa had its own versions of Aesop's fables along the lines of *Why Wart Hog Is So Ugly* and *How Zebra Got His Stripes*. These tales, passed from generation to generation are humorous vehicles for teaching moral lessons. Take for instance, the charming Bantu tale of the Tortoise and the Lizard. Tortoise who had acquired some salt was dragging it behind him on a string because he was the wrong shape to carry it. Lizard jumped on the parcel and laid claim to it because he said it was just lying on the ground. When the case came up before the court of elders, Tortoise argued strongly that as the salt was attached to him by a string it belonged to him. The old men discussed the matter for days but as many of them were related to Lizard and thought they might get a share of the salt they decreed that the bundle should be cut in half. Tortoise who thought this was an unjust outcome bided his time until one day he was able to capture Lizard from behind. "What are you doing?" cried out Lizard. "I was just walking along the path when I found something lying there," explained Tortoise. "So I picked it up and now it belongs to me, just as you picked up my salt the other day." When they went to court the old men listened attentively to both sides of the story before saying, "If we are to be perfectly fair, we must give the same judgement that we gave concerning the salt. Therefore we must cut the lizard in two and Tortoise shall have half."

We were taught to eat with cutlery which was stored in a wooden canteen lined with green felt that my parents had received as a wedding present. Our food would not have disgraced an English nursery. We had shepherd's pie, macaroni cheese, omelettes and baked beans. Mum's vegetable garden yielded crops of carrots, beans, peas, pumpkins and potatoes. We had marmite, peanut butter and marmalade on toast. Under Mum's tutelage Issa created delicious English puddings. Our favourite: the Queen of Puddings had a baked egg base, a layer of jam and a meringue topping. There were lemon meringue pies, cold and hot soufflés, jellies and fruit salads. We had sponge cakes with butter cream in the middle and white icing on top for our birthdays. The only concession to the tropics was boiled milk which we detested because it had a thick skin and a strong taste. We also ate an anodyne version of curry long before it became a national dish in Britain. Bananas, which were healthy and plentiful, cropped up in various guises as fried fritters, hot with golden syrup or baked in their skins.

Birthdays were very English days for us. The few, but much appreciated presents we received were opened at the breakfast table. Some of these came all the way from England in exciting brown paper parcels tied with string and covered in stamps. Stamp collecting was all the rage in those days so they were never thrown away. Inside were board games, puzzles or books. Granny Phillips had a knack of choosing exactly the right gifts. For a few years she sent me little animals made out of glass which grew into an attractive collection before inevitably getting smashed somewhere along the line. She gave me my first wrist watch which in those days was a precious item. Later, for my thirteenth birthday she sent me *Gone with the Wind* which had a visceral emotional impact on me such as I have never since experienced from a book. In the afternoon we had a proper birthday party with as many European children as could be mustered from miles around. We had brightly coloured jellies, and ice-cream which tasted of the vanilla-scented milk powder from which it was made. Then Issa brought in a sponge cake decorated with pink and white icing. *Happy Birthday* was sung and the candles blown out. After tea we played games which were not at all like our make-up African games. We played *Oranges and Lemons, The Farmer's in his Den, Blind Man's Buff*, musical bumps and pass-the-parcel. Mum had a gift for organising amusing parties and we were probably correct in thinking that ours were the best in the district.

As children we had the most disgusting illnesses and maladies which have left me with a lifelong fear of needles and doctors. Malaria was a real hazard and had to be avoided at all costs. It causes fever, high temperature, sweats and delirium and is a most debilitating disease, if it doesn't kill first. The journals of the early European explorers are filled with descriptions of the dreaded fever which would strike them down for weeks and leave them permanently weakened. Today it is still a killer disease dispatching over a million Africans every year. Even the mantle of the "thirteenth orphan" could not shield me from the bitter quinine tablets which we had to swallow daily as a prophylactic against it. No matter how cunningly Mum disguised them they were hard to swallow. She would wrap them in raisins, or crush them in jam. She would beg and bribe me to swallow them, usually to no avail. She would end up by dosing me as she did the dogs – by forcing my jaw open and popping the pill at the back of my throat and clamping my mouth shut until I had swallowed it. Mum's bullying turned out to be a blessing. I know my father suffered recurring bouts of fever over the years. I do not remember me or my sisters getting malaria but Ursula Lewis-Barned told me she remembered an occasion when one of us was in bed with it.

Mum had to dose us (and the dogs) for worms as well. We got a lot of worms because we liked walking around with bare feet in African style and they burrowed through the skin. These parasites enter the body as tiny eggs before hatching into adult worms in the intestines. If not treated, they cause anaemia or worse. Hookworm, flatworm and roundworm – we got them all. But the worst was tapeworm. Tapeworms have heads that attach to the intestinal lining. White and ribbon-like they grew so long that they sometimes hung out of our bottoms. One of the things that freaked us out about having worms was the knowledge that they were stealing our partly digested food and making us hungry. The most common parasites of all were jiggers which usually grew under the skin or nails, often in the big toe, causing the flesh to swell and throb. It was at this moment they needed to be removed before they were given the chance to develop into maggots. This was done with a sewing needle which had been disinfected in a match flame. We made a terrible song and dance about it. At least I know I did. We preferred to let our African servants perform the little operation because they had the knack of doing it more painlessly than Mum. Jiggers were endemic amongst the Africans who mostly went barefoot. Many of them had toes deformed by large growths caused by jigger infections.

Insect bites and scratches easily turned septic in the tropics and despite lashings of TCP and Dettol we were invariably covered with pus-filled sores. I have a hard white scar 3cm in diameter from an infected smallpox vaccination. One of the worst childhood infections I had was impetigo which is a highly contagious skin infection that produces blisters or sores on the face. Today it is easily treated with antibiotic cream but when I was a child the cure was primitive. The weeping sores would be allowed to dry out and develop crusts. These would then have to be torn off to let the healing process renew itself. And on and on this went for weeks. To add insult to

injury the sores were covered with Gentian Violet liquid disinfectant that stained the skin bright purple. I screamed like a banshee
and had to be held down during the scab scraping.

When we lived in Biharamulo Mum attended to all our minor
accidents and ailments. Sunburn was an occupational hazard
because we hated wearing hats and sunscreen cream was unknown.
The cure for this was lashings of calamine lotion which felt blissfully
cool on the skin and smelt delicious. She also dealt with the injuries
and illnesses of local Africans who sat patiently in long queues in the
boma waiting for her attention. She seemed to work wonders with
Eno's Fruit Salts, aspirin, quinine, eye ointment, zinc ointment,
iodine and dressings. We did however have to visit a proper doctor
for our annual jabs. The annual TAB injection, to inoculate us
against tuberculosis and typhoid became a dreaded event in our
lives. The injection itself was just bearable but the after-effects lasted
for a week and were very painful. Mum had a theory that the stiffness
in the arm could be avoided if we moved it vigorously. She made us
play tennis or do arm exercises after the jabs.

As small children in Biharamulo we were physically and emotionally attached to our African servants in whose company we spent
more time than with our parents. Swahili was our first language and
so we had no difficulty communicating with them. They were kind
and caring to children: they would watch out for us, pick us up
when we fell and carry us around when we were tired. Pedro, the
dhobi was especially patient. We liked to watch him doing the
ironing with a big heavy iron which was heated with burning
charcoal. He would make the base fizz when he spat on it to make
sure it was hot enough. No electrical iron can match that smoul-
dering clean smell. The only one who could be grumpy or inclined
to reprimand was Issa who did not like to be disturbed in his
kitchen kingdom.

Our *ayah,* Sofia was solid and calm and never far away. She was
inclined to pinch our arms when we were naughty but she never
slapped us or lost her temper. It was a special treat to be taken to
her hut in the servants' quarters out of sight of the house. We were
fascinated by the women's hairdressing sessions which frequently
took place there. With the aid of a wooden comb and nimble
fingers short frizzy African hair could be woven into intricate rows
and patterns which I envied. Sometimes we had bananas roasted in
the embers of a cooking fire and once we shared in a feast of

Sofia, Julia & Harriet

roasted flying ants which Africans consider a delicate seasonal treat. We ate them in our fingers. They were crunchy and tasted of burnt toast. Sofia lived in a round mud hut with a pointed thatched roof. Inside was a bed made of a wooden frame and leather thongs, an upturned crate, a chair and a curtain which divided the room in two. It was dark inside and smelt smoky and stuffy. The cooking was done on a heap of stones outside the hut. When we moved to Mwanza in 1949 we left Sofia and Pedro behind. Only faithful Issa and his family accompanied us to our new posting. As pre-teenagers and teenagers we never got so close to our African servants again.

As we didn't play much with the African *totos* and there were no other white children close by we had to rely on each other's company. We had the usual sibling squabbles and minded about equal shares and fairness, but on the whole we got on pretty well. Although we were close in age, our characters were very different. Jane was a chubby cheerful toddler. Like many youngest children she fitted in without fuss and was seldom out of sorts. The smiley Buddha-like photos of her at this stage do not seem to have much to do with the clever, competent, slightly severe adult she has become. Harriet was equable and good natured most of the time. She was physically robust and athletic but had a tender emotional streak inside; if hurt or offended she became sulky, she could also be stubborn if so minded. I was the mischief-maker and attention-seeker, a role often adopted by middle siblings. The Africans called me *shungura* after the nimble little rock hyrax.

Julia, Jane & Harriet

Harriet had a remarkable affinity with animals in a way that I never did. She caused a sensation one term at boarding school by managing to conceal a white mouse inside her clothes for a whole term without being spotted. She was not so successful in concealing the mice in the holidays however. When they had babies, which they frequently did, Dad would ignore her pleading and drown them. Animals were always as much part of the family as we were. We loved hearing Mum's story about the beloved terrier she had when Harriet was born: he was so jealous of the new baby that he sulked and skulked around for months. Mum was highly amused when she went to put Harriet to sleep in the pram to find the faithful dog lying there with his head on the pillow. He came round in the end and would not let any stranger near the baby. The first dogs I knew were white bull terriers. They were gentle with members of the household but fought with other dogs and liked to run down African goats and cattle if given half a chance. If they were caught in the act Dad beat them with a hippo-hide stick called a *kiboko*. We blocked our ears and crouched out of sight and simply hated him when he did this despite his reasonable explanation. "I know you think I'm harsh to whip the dogs but I am doing them a favour. They must be taught a lesson they will not forget. If their instincts get the upper hand and they become killers they will have to be put down, if the Africans don't poison them first. Sometimes it is necessary to be harsh to be kind."

Our cats were pale grey Siamese, the old-fashioned kind that is no longer bred. They had squint eyes and a marked kink in the tail. The oldest one Stumpy followed Harriet around like a dog and was allowed to sleep on her bed. One of the many occasions in which I was in disgrace was when I cut off great chunks of his fur coat with a pair of scissors. He disappeared under Harriet's bed and didn't emerge for days, during which time Harriet refused to speak to me. Mum joined in the reprimand by saying, "You've offended his dignity. How would you like it if I cut off all your hair?" Mum was our hairdresser and I did get very upset if she cut my fringe crooked or too short. Despite this I could not resist having a go at Pixie Pickford's handsome head of hair some years later. She was Harriet's best school friend and was staying with us during a summer holiday. Since I hacked the hair off while it was braided in two thick plaits the result was a mangled mess.

The difference between Harriet and me when it came to animals was that she was prepared to do all the boring maintenance jobs like grooming and picking off the ticks. The latter was a task for which I had very little appetite. Whenever the dogs returned from walks in the undergrowth they would be covered in brown and grey ticks which had burrowed under their fur and were gorging on their blood. These had to be plucked off and disposed of in a tin of paraffin. If one detached them intact it could be quite satisfying but more often than not they squashed between our fingers. Mum could relate to Harriet's passion for animals but did draw the line when she was found on her hands and knees eating out of a dog's bowl.

Lake Province was tsetse fly country so Mum was not able to keep a horse. My parents were very afraid of sleeping sickness. African trypanosomiasis is a parasitic disease transmitted by the tsetse fly which is a large brown biting insect that lives by feeding on the blood of vertebrate animals. In humans, the first symptoms are headaches, fevers and joint pains. As the disease develops it causes swollen lymph glands and finally, when it affects the brain, it reverses sleep patterns causing fatigue and sleepiness in the day and insomnia at night. Young though we were we knew about sleeping sickness because several times a year a team of agricultural researchers would visit the *boma* to check up on the various measures such as bush clearance that were being taken to eliminate it.

We had very few toys. In fact for the duration of the war no parcels reached us at all. The only toy I can recollect having had, under the age of six, was a big wooden cart with wheels and a handle that had been constructed for us by a local Indian *fundi*. For play we had all the ingredients provided by nature. And very creative we were with these. The only time we were bored was when we were trapped in cars or lorries on long journeys. We had crazes which captivated us for weeks. There was the funeral craze when we killed beetles and insects before burying them in elaborate ceremonies which involved making twig crosses and sprinkling petals on the graves. We were always trying to catch basking lizards to see if they escaped by leaving their tails behind them. There was the pottery craze when we pulverised richly coloured stones to make clay which we fashioned into crude objects. We made plates and baskets out of banana leaves. We made scent by crushing eucalyptus leaves and distilling them in hot water. We constructed houses in trees, under bushes or in the long grass. Mum, who was sometimes called upon to judge the best, had a judicious way of awarding out three first prizes along the lines of: "Harriet's is constructed best. Julia's is the most original and Jane's is the tidiest."

Some of our escapades were not so well received. I am afraid that I was the ring leader of an adventure that gained myth-like proportions. The DO's house in Biharamulo had been built by the Germans before 1914. Sturdily constructed of stone with buttresses and a round tower, it was more fortification than house. It was enclosed in a high walled courtyard which contained the *boma* buildings. In one corner there was access, via a buttress, to the sloping corrugated iron roof. The endeavour of clambering up the buttress onto the roof by a six year-old, a four-year-old (me) and a

two-year-old must have been herculean. But clamber up we did, and for good measure we decided to do it in the nude. We hauled our wooden cart up after us, and popped Jane inside it. Harriet and I then drew the cart up to the pinnacle of the roof and let it go until it reached the edge, whereupon, with whoops and yells, we dashed to retrieve it. Jane gurgled and waved her plump little arms with glee. As the game continued word got about and a crowd of office workers gathered in the courtyard below. Horrified though they were my parents had the good sense not to call out lest we got distracted and let go of the cart. Instead, a couple of Africans crept up onto the roof and grabbed us from behind. We were not punished, but Dad's cold disapproval addressed to Harriet and I was punishment enough.

"That was an extremely silly game. If you had lost your grip on the cart you would have sent your sister to her death."

"But it was such fun" I protested.

"Putting other people's lives in danger is no joke. And what on earth possessed you to take your clothes off?"

"Julia said it would make us invisible" Harriet explained.

"And did you become invisible? Of course not. You must learn to be less gullible in future."

"What's gullible?" asked Harriet in a small voice.

"A fish that goes for bait and swallows a hook is gullible" Dad replied.

I can clearly recall the few occasions when Dad lost his temper.

His outbursts were less frequent but more considered than Mum's squalls. One was early on Christmas day when we draped ourselves in sheets and uttering ghostly cries burst into our parents' bedroom while they were asleep. Dad was so irritated that he smacked our bottoms. Another was when we were travelling by train. We were chugging along with the window open when I got an irresistible urge and acted on it. I darted forward, whipped Dad's solar topee off his head and hurled it out of the train window. Once he had got over his astonishment he laid me across his knees and gave me a sound smack. These admonishments seemed fair enough and caused no resentment.

When we were not being physically active we read, played cards and board games (like Monopoly) and listened to music. Our gramophone and piano were precious family possessions. The wooden gramophone was cranked up by a handle and had a curved bronze head for the needle which needed to be placed by hand on the edge of the vinyl 78 record. The piano was a small brown upright which was generally badly out of tune for lack of an expert to tune it. It folded up for travelling and followed my father through his postings. He was a self-taught musician and had a fine baritone voice. I never tired of hearing him sing *One Fish Ball*. He delivered the ridiculous words with expression and bathos. This poor gentleman entered a fancy restaurant with fifteen cents in his pocket. After scanning the menu he called the waiter down the hall and softly whispered, "one fish ball.' Here my father's voice fell to a whisper. 'The waiter bellowed down the hall, "This gentleman here wants one fish ball!". Here my father bellowed. The punch line was everything a young child could wish for. "The wretched man then went outside and shot himself until he died." Another great favourite was *Abdul the Bulbul Ameer* but alas I do not remember the words of this.

Nothing delighted my father more than a musical evening. He could accompany himself up to a point, but for the scores of his beloved Gilbert and Sullivan he had to rely on a good pianist. In Biharamulo this service was spasmodically provided by one of the White Fathers from the mission at Katohe five miles away. We loved it when these neighbouring priests paid us a visit. They were so friendly and jolly. We liked it when they kissed us because their thick beards were tickly. Their long white robes did not deter them from riding about on motorcycles. These good men did appreciate a real English tea of egg sandwiches, scones and fruitcake which Issa provided without having to be told. They would bring a bottle of their home-distilled orange liqueur which fuelled the jovial atmosphere. We were allowed to stay up late and join in the singing. It was a sad day when the parent house found out about the visits and stopped them coming to our home.

Chapter 10

Stanley and Livingstone

In the tradition of pride in the British Empire we were brought up on tales of two great white African explorers, David Livingstone and Henry Morton Stanley. They were better known to us than Raleigh or Drake. My father was fascinated by the C19 explorations in Africa. Their exploits make exciting reading for anyone, but for someone familiar (as my father was) with the weather, the topography and the vastness of Africa these exploits were more than exciting, they were remarkable. The story we loved best was when Stanley found Livingstone in Ujiji on the eastern shore of Lake Tanganyika in November 1871. It went like this:

David Livingstone had become famous after he had crossed the whole of Africa along the Zambezi river between 1863 and 1865. In 1866 he returned to East Africa in search of the source of the Nile but disappeared into the interior for so long that no one knew whether he was alive or dead. In the meantime Henry Morton Stanley an ambitious adventurer-cum-journalist, had persuaded the *New York Herald* to fund him in a search for Dr Livingstone. The three-month journey in 1871 was a baptism of fire for the man who was to become the most famous explorer of the century. His two white companions died en route. He became involved in a war between Arab traders and an African tribe. Many of his bearers either died or deserted and he himself suffered several bouts of severe malaria. He despaired of finding Livingstone dead or alive.

Fortunately for his future reputation, Stanley did eventually find him. The meeting, as recounted to us children, was as follows. It was with growing anticipation and excitement that Stanley and his followers drew near to Lake Tanganyika. They had received reports of the presence of a white man in the village of Ujiji. When they were within reach of the village volleys of shot were fired. At the head of the column was an *askari* carrying an American flag.

Alongside him came Stanley, dressed in a freshly pressed flannel suit, white solar topee and oiled knee boots. An emaciated old man in a navy cap, old red waistcoat and grey tweed trousers came out of a hut to greet him. Stanley, with arm outstretched then uttered the immortal words: "Dr Livingstone I presume?"

This greeting later became known the world over. When Stanley returned to Britain after his encounter with Livingstone, he found to his dismay and astonishment that he was both patronised and ridiculed for it. In some instances he was publicly disbelieved. In fact, the establishment, especially the Royal Geographical Society was very grudging in its welcome, at least initially. The irony, as I have since discovered, was that Stanley, in an effort to dramatise the meeting, had invented these words for his dispatches to the *New York Herald*. In reality the meeting seems to have been both more prosaic and charming. Livingstone's faithful servant Susi had come rushing to meet them with the greeting, "How do you do, Sir."

"Who the deuce are you?" enquired Stanley.

"I am Susi the servant of Dr Livingstone."

"Now, you Susi, run and tell the doctor I am coming."

They enjoyed each other's company and parted with regret. When he said goodbye to Livingstone, who refused to accompany him, Stanley had a presentiment that he would never see him alive again. He was right about that. Livingstone died thirteen months later near Lake Bangweulu. Chuma and Susi, his loyal African followers then undertook a journey, every bit as extraordinary as their master's. They removed Livingstone's heart and buried it under a tree. They dried and preserved his body, wrapped it in tarred sailcloth and proceeded to carry it, on poles, all the way to the coast. They had to cross the Luapula River, wade through swamps, fend off lions and fight their way out of a hostile village. When they reached Tabora they bumped into an expedition led by Lieutenant Cameron who had been sent out to find Livingstone. Cameron wanted the body of Livingstone to be buried on the spot, but Chuma and Susi bravely insisted that it was Livingtone's last wish to be buried at home in England. So their extraordinary journey to the coast continued. Nine months after they set off, they laid the body and a bundle containing stubs of pencil, journals, a bible, sextant and compass and a red shirt at the doorway of the Christian chapel in Bagamoyo. From here it was transported back home. Had it not been for Stanley's best-selling book, *How I Met*

Livingstone, the explorer might have died in comparative obscurity, but Stanley's account ensured the doctor's reputation as a great explorer and a saintly man. Stanley was one of his pall bearers at the magnificent funeral that was arranged for him at Westminster Abbey.

Julia, Jane & Harriet

All this was very thrilling stuff and led indirectly to an episode in our early childhood that nearly ended in disaster. When we lived in Biharamulo the *bundu* (bush) which was close to the *boma* was strictly out of bounds. The tall grass studded with shrubs and queerly shaped thorn trees was asking to be explored. I wasn't quite brave enough to explore it by myself. Stanley had always taken along assistants on his explorations and despite the fact that most of them had perished on his explorations it seemed logical that I should have assistants myself. This matter took some time to arrange. Harriet was not in the least frightened of the bush because animals, even wild ones, held no terror for her. But she did not like being disobedient so I had a hard time persuading her that when we had succeeded in opening up the unknown territory beyond the banana grove, Mum and Dad would be so proud of us that they would forget to be cross. Jane was unmoved by the example of the famous explorers and was not keen on walking. In the end though, she was not prepared to be left behind.

The day of departure was carefully chosen. Sofia, our ayah, had gone to a neighbouring village to visit a sick relative. Mum was occupied in the *boma*. It was Pedro's washing day and father had gone up country in the car with Issa. He had taken the dogs with him. Unlike Stanley, who had taken a huge amount of luggage with him on his journey into the interior, we had no porters and no supplies. I had managed to sneak a tin of sticking plaster out of the First Aid box and a ball of string from Dad's desk. We intended to live off the fruits of the land, but for emergencies only I had brought along a pot of marmite from the storeroom. Our clothes were most unsuitable. We should have been wearing khaki safari suits and knee-high leather mosquito boots but since we didn't have any we had to make do with the red and white cotton sundresses and sandals we were standing up in. I insisted, however, that we wore our miniature solar topees.

"But you are always the first to take your sunhat off when Mum's back is turned" Harriet complained.

"Today is different" was my retort, "we are going on a long journey and we may die of sunstroke if we don't wear hats".

"I don't want a long journey," whined Jane. "I want Sofia".

"We are going to look for her" I promised cunningly.

At last we were ready. I led the way with a walking stick purloined from my father's collection to ward off snakes. Jane toiled after me while Harriet, carrying a string bag with water and marmite brought up the rear. It was about 9 a.m and the sun was climbing in the clear blue sky. By midday it would be overhead and very hot. We tripped gaily through our own garden with its abundant red cannas, orange marigolds and white daisies. We went down the hill, past a cluster of African huts until we came to the banana grove. Here, Stumpy the cat who had been faithfully stalking Harriet turned round for home. Not being as wise as he, we pressed on through the grove. The huge shiny green leaves of the banana trees made a roof over our heads through which the sun came in dappled rays. We picked some low-hanging bananas but they were hard and green and made our teeth feel furry. When we emerged from the grove the sun was so bright we had to blink hard to adjust to it.

Jane started to complain. She wasn't used to walking and her fat little legs were aching. But there was no turning back now. For a time I kept her going with bribes. "I'll tell you stories every night for a whole year". When this had no effect I told her that Sofia would carry her home. Finally, I threatened to leave her behind to be eaten by lions. But in the end even horror stories had no more power over her. She sat down on the ground and howled. We temporarily pacified her by allowing her to stick her finger in the marmite pot. After fortifying ourselves with water and marmite (which made us thirstier than ever) we set out with Jane riding piggyback on Harriet. Up until then we had been following a faint and meandering footpath through the tall elephant grass. This now petered out and the going became much more difficult. It was quite impossible to go forward in a straight line because there was always a rocky outcrop, a thorn tree or a distorted anthill to be negotiated. Our bare legs got badly scratched; our arms got sunburnt and horse flies stung us without mercy. The bush was a noisy place. Hidden grasshoppers rasped their legs together, and exotic birds screeched out danger. Human voices (apart from our own) were noisily absent.

"I can't go another step" groaned Harriet, gently laying Jane, who had gone to sleep, on the ground before sitting wearily down besides her. A few seconds later she jumped up with a scream and started to caper madly round in circles. She had disturbed an army of *siafu* (large safari ants) who were on the march and had got ants in her pants. I threw down the stick and rushed to her aid. "Keep still" I commanded as I tried to pick ants off her body.

"That's it" she said firmly when free of her tormentors. "I'm going home with or without you."

"I don't want to be standinlivingroom any longer" Jane seconded. "I want my Mummy."

Harriet could be very stubborn and I knew I was stumped. I looked round for the *boma* so that I could get my bearings. It was nowhere to be seen. All I could see was bush stretching as far as the eye could see. I began to feel frightened but did not want the others to know so I struck off in what I hoped was the right direction. We plodded miserably on and on in the fierce sunshine until Harriet noticed an anthill that we had passed earlier on. Anthills have the most extraordinary shapes and no one anthill is like another. "I think we are going round in circles" I meekly admitted. "You mean we are lost? I nodded. It was too much. We clung together sobbing with despair. We collapsed on a bare patch of ground under a spiky thorn tree. We had finished the water and had no appetite for the marmite. It was growing cooler and we knew that night would fall very suddenly without warning. It did and we began to think of the wild animals that came out of hiding when it was dark. Then we heard a sound we knew well. It was the laughing bark of a hyena. Hyenas are bold creatures that hunt in packs and would come right up to the house at night. We often heard them and saw their white turds in the morning. The sound set Janie off again. "The *fisi* are coming to eat me up" she sobbed and could not be comforted. My teeth began to chatter with fear. I recalled the words of the sad song that Mum often sang to us: *The Poor Babes in the Wood* about two children who got lost in a forest and never woke up. I believed that we would never wake again, only instead of little birds covering us gently with leaves as per the tender illustration in the book of nursery rhymes, hungry lions would tear the flesh off our bones. Eventually we cried ourselves to sleep.

We were woken up by sounds of shouting, whistling and barking. The night sky was brightly lit by stars and a sliver of moon. We jumped up and began shouting in unison. The bull terriers were the first on the scene. When they had knocked us over in exuberance, our parents came into view. They were followed by Issa, Pedro and dozens of villagers carrying flaming torches. We were picked up with hugs and kisses and carried home on strong black shoulders. We were bathed and fed hot ovaltine and biscuits. Our scratches and insect bites were treated with disinfectant and our sunburn soothed with calamine lotion. When we were finally tucked up in bed under our mosquito nets Mum came in to kiss us goodnight. "You walked miles and miles" she told us. "It was a miracle that you were wearing red and white dresses. I spotted a glimpse of scarlet through the binoculars just before darkness fell. Otherwise we might not have found you until daybreak."

"I don't want to be standinlivingroom anymore" muttered Jane sleepily.

"Oh! So that's what set you off." Mum looked sharply in my direction as if to say she knew I had been the ringleader all along. "Well, let me tell you one thing, Stanley and Livingstone would never have set of without telling someone where they were going."

When I cast my mind back to my early childhood I realise that it was full of dramatic incidents. On one occasion I became disorientated in a crowd of Africans when I became detached from the family group for a short time, maybe in a market place or during some local ceremony. With a growing sense of panic I began darting about – searching for white people. All of a sudden I bumped into a white man. But when I looked up at him I got a terrible fright; he had the whitest skin imaginable, yellowish-white hair and pink eyes. Yet his hair and features were manifestly African. I am not quite sure exactly what it was that caused me to become hysterical. Maybe it was the incongruity. When I was reunited with my family, and was able to articulate what had happened, my parents explained that he was an albino. An explanation of albinism as a genetic deficiency of the pigment would have meant nothing, but their rational tone of voice calmed me down. I did have nightmares of the incident for a while, though in the end Mum's advice got through. "You should feel sorry for him, not scared of him. Imagine how miserable he would be if everyone who meets him started screaming." What my parents did not reveal at the time was that this individual was lucky to have reached adulthood alive. Albino babies tended to be murdered and their body parts used in witchcraft.

I was also terrified of lepers who were supposed to live as outcasts in leper colonies but sometimes went begging for alms when they were no longer infectious. They might be missing fingers, arms, legs or bits of their faces. These disfigurements together with the rags they wore gave them a frightening appearance. Again my parents tried to reassure us that they were human beings like the rest of us but I dreaded bumping into them.

We girls had an unusual bedroom in our semi-fortified home in Biharamulo. We slept in a round tower, up a staircase that was slightly detached from the rest of the house. The room was barely furnished with three beds, shelves for books and clothes. The chart of English monarchs was tacked to a wall. The feet of the beds stood in their empty tobacco tins filled with paraffin, the mosquito nets on round hoops hung from the ceiling above each bed. Once we were tucked up for the night Mum would come up with a pressure lamp to read us stories. When she left the room the only light came from a flickering hurricane lamp left on the bookshelf. We were used to the sounds of the wild as we drifted off to sleep: the whining of mosquitoes, the barking of hyenas and the hooting of owls. But one dark night we were woken by an unfamiliar bumping, scraping noise that came from inside rather than outside the house. When I opened my eyes I saw a dark brooding figure on the end of Harriet's bed. It looked human and yet somehow not human. Round luminous eyes were suspended where a head should have been. It could only be one thing – Dracula come to suck our blood. Our concerted screaming brought our parents rushing to the tower. Before we had time to explain what had terrified us, my father exclaimed, "Well I'm damned look at that owl."

"He's gigantic" Mum said. "How on earth did he get in?"

"Please, please take him away. It's Dracula come to suck our blood" I begged.

"We will have to trap him in a blanket" Dad suggested. "He's got a wicked beak." "Poor thing," mused Mum. "He's probably as frightened as the girls."

Removing the huge creature was easier said than done. Dad moved cautiously round the room until he was behind the owl, before darting forward with a blanket which he threw over it: the owl struggled violently. His claws made a din on the floor. My father pinioned him inside the blanket, carried him to a window and pushed him out still wrapped in the blanket. He broke free from his wrapping in mid air and flew away with a loud flapping of wings. Mum had to read us a lot of *Uncle Remus* stories before we were able to go back to sleep.

My early childhood can best be summed up in the words of Charles Allen quoted in *Plain Tales from the Raj*. "I grew up in bright sunshine, I grew up with tremendous space, I grew up with animals, I grew up with excitement, I grew up believing that white people were superior."

Chapter 11

Mwanza

When I was eight years old we moved to Mwanza with some of our animals. We had two Siamese cats called Why and What. Our bull terriers did not take to town life so they were replaced by a tan coloured dachshund called Cha Cha who in no time produced two mongrel puppies called High and Low. Best of all we acquired a donkey called Long Ears. After the isolation of Biharamulo, we considered Mwanza to be the height of sophistication with its proper shops, hospital, church, hotel, stone houses, port and jetties. Most exotic of all was the cinema nick-named the Fleapit. My own children can't recall the first film they ever saw, having had a surfeit at a young

Julia on Long Ears

age. But for me, the first picture (which was what a movie was called then) *Annie Get Your Gun* was indelibly printed on my memory. I knew every word of every song and must have bored my parents to distraction with oft-repeated performances. The club was, as usual, the focus of expat social and sporting life. Harriet and I were keen tennis players and there were frequent tournaments in which we competed. We were thrilled to find European children of our own age with whom we quickly became friends. We would dash about in groups making free with each other's houses.

We lived in two houses in Mwanza. The first one was in a European neighbourhood right on the lake. Hippos would stomp up from the water in the evenings and trample the flowerbeds and lawns. From here Dad would ride Long Ears to the office. The donkey turned out to be a bit of a disappointment. He was bad tempered, his backbone was sharp and his mouth was as hard as nails. The only person who could ride him with any degree of comfort was Dad who knotted his long legs under the donkey's stomach and kept him in line with a stick.

We left this house when my father became acting Provincial Commissioner to take up residence in a fascinating abode. It had been built by the Germans as a mini schloss in a strategic position on top of a rocky outcrop in the middle of town. From it we had a perfect view of Bismarck Rock, a balancing rock formation that stands like a sentinel in the water of the ferry harbour. To reach the house we had to leave the car at the bottom and walk up a steep path. This hike was enlivened by the antics of the cheeky grey monkeys who inhabited the encroaching rocks and trees. We learnt

from experience that it was a mistake to give them snacks on the way up. Once, when we dispensed some bananas, we were mobbed by troupes of aggressive animals who advanced on us with bared teeth and chattering cries. We were forced to keep them at bay by brandishing our tennis racquets. Although we had wire netting on the doors and windows they would frequently nip into the house in search of food. We spent happy hours climbing and exploring the rocks surrounding the house, a habitat that was shared by hyraxes, colourful agama lizards, snakes and wild cats.

We were very proud when my father became deputy Provincial Commissioner and was entitled to stick a Union Jack on the bonnet of our battered grey Ford car. During the school holidays our parents involved us in their official entertainments. We were

allowed to appear for drinks before dinner parties. If they were giving a cocktail party we carried round the plates of toasties. Like most children we could spot the adults who were genuinely interested in what we had to say. The three of us got a spanking on one memorable social occasion. We were supposed to be on our best behaviour while Mum was giving tea to an African chief. He was smartly dressed in an embroidered *kanzu* and beaded hat and was carrying a fly whisk. Mum asked me to offer the chief a chocolate éclair. To our great dismay he retained the plate on his knee and polished off the lot. Not to be outdone, our greedy dachshund Cha Cha waddled over for her share whereupon the chief picked her up by the scruff of the neck. At her shrill squeal of protest we burst into giggles and could not stop. When Dad, who had been delayed at the office turned up, Mum managed to intercept him before he came into the room. He greeted the chief before banishing us with the ominous words, "Wait outside. I'll deal with you later." The chief brought a spotted handkerchief to his mouth to hide his smile as chastened we filed out of the room. Dad dealt with us by beating our bottoms with a tennis shoe with the injunction never to be rude to someone who is ignorant of one's ways.

In Mwanza, my father found a pearl without price in the shape of a Scottish woman of outstanding musical ability. Winifred Ramsay was dark, tall and willowy. She had huge brown eyes, a mobile face, a strong articulated Scottish accent and an infectious laugh. She was a professional violinist and talented music teacher. She had come out to Tanganyika at the age of 22 with her older husband who was an irrigation engineer. She was a vivacious personality with limitless energy and threw herself into colonial life. She patched up her violin which had been damaged in transit and began to teach violin and singing in schools and in the community. In all her postings which were numerous, she formed madrigal groups, choirs and small orchestras. There were many Scots serving in colonial departments such as agriculture, railways, prisons and education as well as hospitals and Win was always the life and soul of the Scottish dancing and Caledonian societies. She believed that there was music in everybody if only it could be accessed, though she had to admit that this did not apply to her husband Jack. Win and Jack became my parents' closest friends and we girls were fond of the two Ramsay boys, Alasdair and Euan.

Musical evenings became a weekly ritual. Mum would organise the meal, Jack would do any intricate handiwork that needed attention like mending cutlery, and Win would coach my father from the piano. Initially Win rather looked down on Gilbert and Sullivan but before long she was gustily singing duets with Dad. We girls were encouraged to sing along. When the two families went out for expeditions in the government launch on Lake Victoria, Dad would bring along musical scores and we would take different parts. I have only to hear music from a Gilbert and Sullivan opera to be transported back to those halcyon days. Harriet, Jane and I made a party piece out of *Three Little Maids from School* (The Mikado); Dad's were the Major General from *The Pirates of Penzance* and The Lord Chancellor from *HMS Pinafore*. Win produced several amateur Gilbert and Sullivan operas in which my father played lead roles. He loved performing in public which was surprising for someone so reserved. By the end of her time in Tanganyika in the late fifties, Win had moved to Dar and was conducting a

multi-racial orchestra. She had Indians playing stringed instruments and Africans from the King's African Rifles providing the
brass. She also coached African girls' choirs. If Win was working in
Africa today I am sure she would have immersed herself in the
indigenous musical tradition. At this epoch few Europeans appreciated the intense rhythm, drums and song of the Africans.

I am filled with amazement at the physical freedom we had in
Mwanza. We would ride our bikes wherever we wanted, including
out of town. We took picnics and went out all day exploring on the
rocky outcrops or in the bush. There was no question of heeding
strangers or avoiding Africans. Mum would give us two warnings:
"Don't go near a stray dog and run away if you see a snake." She did
not have to warn us. We were very afraid of being bitten by a rabid
dog. We had heard that victims went mad and foamed at the mouth
before dying of thirst. Worse still, treatment involved injections in
the stomach. We were habitually afraid of snakes and had always
hated using long-drop lavatories in case snakes were coiled under
the wooden seats. We knew that we should run whenever we saw a
snake without stopping to find out if it was poisonous or not.
Snakes don't usually attack unless disturbed but as they like to sun
themselves and are so well camouflaged it was easy to step on them.
One of our dogs had died from a puff adder's bite and once in the
garden at Biharamulo we had seen a deadly cobra rise up from its
coils with its hood spread out preparing to spit its deadly load. We
ran screaming for help, but by the time the *shamba* boy had
returned with a heavy knife called a *panga* the cobra had slithered
away.

We had two encounters with the mighty python, a snake that can
grow to six metres in length and can squeeze an antelope to death.
Mum and Dad were out walking in the bush with Cha Cha when
they realized that she was no longer following them. On retracing
their footsteps they found her suffocating in the coils of a huge
python. Her eyes were bulging and her tongue had turned black
and swollen. While Mum ran off to raise a shotgun, Dad set about
beating the snake's head with the wooden walking stick he always
carried with him. He managed to stun the snake and extricate the
poor dog. When Mum returned with a shotgun he shot it. Cha Cha
not only made a full recovery but retained her enormous sex
appeal. She produced so many litters that I imagine half the dogs
in Lake Province contain a trace of her DNA. She lived to the ripe

old age of eighteen. Mum had the python skin dried, cured and made into a pair of shoes. I was not entirely happy about these shoes because having read H.H Munro's *Rikki Tikki Tavi* I feared that the python's mate might come looking for revenge. The second incident happened to a friend called William who had been swimming in a waterhole when he was grabbed by a water python which fastened its fangs round his ankle. He was rescued and rushed to hospital. When he came out he proudly showed off the tooth marks which resembled a tattooed bracelet. I am sure our shuddering response was all he could have wished for.

Our playground extended into Lake Victoria too, which in retrospect seems even more astonishing. The water was usually as calm and still as a shining mirror but storms and squalls could arise very suddenly, as the explorer Stanley experienced when he was circumnavigating it in his small boat. We were not allowed to swim in the open lake because of the dangers of crocodiles and hippo so were taken swimming some miles out of town to an area of the lake which had been enclosed in iron bars. This facility was for whites only. Africans were left to splash around unprotected and were now and again taken by crocodiles. We were allowed to go boating from the house and spent hours pottering around in a canoe stabilised by side floats. We were not as frightened of hippos as we should have been They could look very alarming when they yawned to reveal cavernous mouths and tusks, but mostly they kept their huge bodies still and cool under water so that with only tiny eyes and ears visible they looked rather innocuous.

We knew perfectly well how lethal crocodiles could be. My

parents were friends with a crocodile hunter who was affectionately called Walky Talky Cooper. This rugged, deeply tanned man earned his living shooting crocodiles and selling their skins. One trip on his boat in the company of a wicked looking baby crocodile

Boating on the Lake

was quite enough for us. More sinister were the bangs and movements of the adult crocodiles who were trapped under the floorboards. Cooper regaled us with stories of extraordinary items he had extricated from the stomachs of his victims over the years. Apart from human bones he had found anchors, *debbies* and chunks of wood.

One of the most exciting books I read as a child was *The Kon-Tiki Expedition* by Thor Hyerdahl. In 1947 this Norwegian explorer had built a copy of a prehistoric craft out of balsa wood logs and with a single sail had taken it from Callao in Peru to an island in Polynesia in 101 days. One holiday I got a gang of friends together to build our own *Kon-Tiki* raft. This involved strenuous labour cutting down trees and lashing them together. We made a sail out of an old sheet. At last, the great day arrived for the launch. The raft was dragged to the shore and shoved into the water. Before we could scramble aboard it had sunk without trace. This was a very sad and disappointing moment, but – in the breadth of its ambition – was typical of the sort of outdoor activities we indulged in.

One consequence of playing around in the lake was that we contracted the potentially serious disease of bilharzia. This is caused by yet another of the horrid tropical parasites which wriggles into the body where it matures and reproduces. Eventually it causes damage to the liver and kidneys. It was diagnosed during some routine experimental tests. It transpired that all three of us had it and may well have done so for a year or more. Treatment involved intravenous injections in our arms. Mum became exasperated at the fuss we made, especially as bilharzia was endemic in the Africans who received no treatment at all. But in our defence I have to say that the injections, even with the help of tourniquets, were hit-and-miss affairs.

The use of the government launch, complete with captain and crew, was a perk of Dad's job. We made wonderful trips on the lake at weekends. Friends, especially the Ramsays, were frequently invited along too. When we were out of sight of land we could dive off the boat in crocodile-free water. We would go to Kigungu, Mbarika, Nyamtukusa and Ukara. The adults would sleep in the cabin and the children on deck. We would have barbeques on sandy beaches or the launch would push through the lush mangrove and papyrus swamps and carpets of water lilies in the narrow finger-like inlets. This was Mum's special treat because it was a paradise for water birds like the Great White Egret, the turquoise Kingfisher, and the dainty Jacana that walk on water lilies. The birds seemed to live in harmony with the crocodiles asleep on the banks. When the crocs were not in motion they lay as still as logs, but when they were after prey or entering the water they could move with surprising speed.

A popular destination for a longer boat trip was Ukerewe Island. The DO of Ukerewe was Neville French. He and his wife Joyce became close friends of my parents. We spent two Christmas holidays with them on the island. They had three children who were younger than us. Dad was god-father to their son Christopher. Neville French went on to become Governor of the Falklands Islands.

It was here in Mwanza that the explorer Stanley again entered our lives. After he had shared his discovery of Livingstone with the world Stanley returned to Africa determined to solve the disputes over the source of the Nile. The 7,000 mile journey he accomplished between November 1874 and August 1877 was incredible. After circumnavigating Lakes Victoria and Tanganyika he was able to prove that the Nile rose in Lake Victoria. He then struggled all the way down the River Congo to the Atlantic coast. The only three white men he chose to accompany him were unknown and from working-class backgrounds. From hundreds of applicants he had picked Frederick Barker who was a clerk in the Langham Hotel where Stanley stayed when in London, and the brothers Francis and Edward Pocock who were fishermen from the Medway.

Edward Pocock died early on in the expedition. When Stanley sailed round Lake Victoria in the *Lady Alice* which had been transported across the country in sections, he had to leave Frank Pocock and Fred Barker behind for lack of space. In his absence, Barker succumbed to fever, died and was buried in Kagehyi. The faithful and indispensable Mabruki who had been on expeditions led by Burton, Speke, Grant and Livingstone also died of dysentery. They were buried under piles of stones near the lake. Two years later a missionary called John Smith was buried close by. By the time we arrived in Mwanza the graves were in very poor condition. Dad made it his mission to restore them. He offered a financial reward to any African who found missing stones in Kagehyi and eventually two of the headstones were re-erected on stone plinths within a small walled cemetery.

For us children the white men were the heroes. We did not pay much attention to the Africans who had made the expeditions possible. They were the ones who carried the precious 40 and 60 pound loads of food, instruments, cloth and beads for barter. They were the ones who hacked through impenetrable forest and waded through crocodile infested streams. They were the ones who defended the camp. When they died, and a huge number of them did, they were either left in the bush to rot, or hastily buried in nameless graves. As a child I never questioned the legitimacy of these expeditions. It was not until I was a university student that I realised how one-sided this view was. In Livingstone's defence it must be said that he played an important part in bringing an end to slavery by informing the world of its terrible effects which he had seen with his own eyes. It seems incredible to think that when Dad first arrived in Tanganyika in 1931, the slave trade had in reality only been eradicated in Africa for some thirty years. There were still people alive who had known Zanzibar when it had been a slave market.

When Dad visited outlying districts in his province he was often entertained by the local chieftain with an *ngoma*. Sometimes, as a treat, he took us along too. These entertainments lasted for hours and it was easy, even for aliens like ourselves, to get swept up in the intense and febrile atmosphere. The rhythm was provided by skilled drummers who were seated on the ground with the drums between their knees. These were made from animal skins tightened across the drum. The drummers beat with the palms of their hands rather than with sticks. Every tribe would have its particular dances and songs. By this time my parents would have gained some knowledge of the *ngoma's* underlying meanings from Hans Cory. Over the years Hans had translated a collection of *ngoma* songs into English. Some are war songs which refer to the arrival of the whites. Others about hunting, courting and competitions are full of humour.

Sometimes the women danced alone, sometimes the men. I remember one dance where the men jumped so high and landed so vigorously that the ground trembled. They were dancing around a central figure in a leopard skin whose head was concealed by a grotesque painted mask surmounted by a magnificent ostrich feather headdress. He moved in quite a different style from the others, swaying and dipping and sweeping his headdress along the ground. Gradually the tempo of the drums increased and the masked figure revolved faster and faster. All at once he fell to the ground and lay quite still, whereupon the dancing and drumming stopped abruptly. Even more impressive was an *ngoma* where the men danced with pythons in their arms. The pythons were drugged and somnolent but the sight of them sent shivers up our spines. The male dancers wore painted blocks under their feet which emphasized the stamping movements of their dancing.

An event that made a great impression on us was the arrival in Mwanza of a holy man from India. He looked old and was very thin – almost skin and bone. He had long grey hair and a straggly grey beard. We called him the Sufi but I think this was incorrect because he wore a wrap-around white garment like Mahatma Ghandi who was a Hindu. Whether he was a conjuror or had a more serious spiritual mission I cannot now surmise but he staged a show of being buried alive for twenty-four hours.

This extraordinary event drew a huge crowd of Africans, Indians and Europeans. A hole was dug in the ground large enough to contain a coffin-like box. After turning around a few times with raised arms to show that he was empty-handed the Sufi laid himself down in the box which had been held up to show that it was empty. An assistant nailed down the lid. The box was lowered in the ground and covered with at least a foot of earth. We girls perched ourselves on high ground from which we could observe the proceedings. Here we stayed put for the whole day – quite a feat of endurance since there was nothing happening. When night fell we had to return home, having received assurance that sentinels would be keeping guard to make sure there was no hanky-panky.

We returned to the site as soon as dawn broke. Lo and behold! At the allotted time the box was dug up and out stepped the Sufi, looking none the worse for having been buried alive. Maybe this guru had mastered the art of shallow breathing or maybe he made use of some conjuring breathing device. In any event, Mum was sufficiently impressed to ask him to tell her fortune. I imagine money must have passed hands for this. He did this with great solemnity by first measuring her shadow and then consulting a large book. At the time I did not pay much attention to his prediction but a few years later when it came true I remembered clearly what he had said: "You will have a serious illness and will cross the water to be healed."

Chapter 12

Dar es Salaam

Our last posting in 1955 to Dar came exactly at the right moment for us girls. The Arab name Dar es Salaam means "Haven of Peace". For teenagers it was a haven of fun. The town had been an Arab trading settlement until it fell into decline and was purchased from the Sultan of Zanzibar by the Imperial German Government who turned it into their capital three years later. The wide sweep of harbour was full of activity as dhows and yachts tacked between the large steam ships. The Germans had erected some fine buildings, including the Town Hall, the High Court, and Ocean Road Hospital. Government House, which was the Governor's residence, was the most imposing building we had ever seen in Africa. It was set in the midst of a garden with an enormous lawn which was kept green with the aid of sprinklers, an unheard of act of lavishness.

Government House

By the time we arrived Dar was a veritable metropolis. Electricity was supplied by a municipal grid and there was a main water supply. To our amazement there was more than one of everything. For instance, there were several street markets, two cinemas, a number of hotels and restaurants, several banks, rows of shops, and numerous mosques and churches. Karimjee Hall was a fine new building where the Legislative Council met. The Askari monument held pride of place. This bronze memorial of an African soldier holding a rifle at the ready was built by the British in 1927 as a belated tribute to the thousands of African soldiers and bearers who lost their lives in WWI. Traffic *askaris* in crisp white uniforms proudly directed unruly cars and buses with exaggerated arm gestures and shrill whistle bursts.

Our last house

Before moving to a house in the town centre we lived in a bungalow in Oyster Bay on the Indian Ocean. This was a popular area for Europeans. It felt very luxurious to have running water, electric light, a flush lavatory in the house and a kitchen next to the dining-room. We could run out of the house, up a tussocky slope and dive straight into the sea. During the school holidays we dashed from one physical activity to another in a gang of congenial friends. Amongst others there was Chris Howes and his brother

Mike, the Seabrook twins, Jeremy Mackenzie, Sandy Forbes and Charmian Ireland. We had unlimited freedom to roam around on our own. We played tennis matches at the Gymkhana Club and learnt to sail at the yacht club. We would swim in Oyster Bay and Leopard's Cove and surf at Kunduchi outside town. Our equipment was unsophisticated. For tennis we had wooden racquets with gut strings, for surfing we used boogie-boards and for snorkelling a mask with a breathing tube. We swam in canvas *tackies* as a protection against sea urchins whose spikes became septic if embedded in the sole of the foot.

Today tourists pay a lot of money to experience the underwater exploring we took completely for granted. We would don flippers and mask and spend hours in an enchanted watery kingdom of coral formations inhabited by exotic and strange fish. We learnt to steer clear of the huge shoals of transparent jellyfish called Portuguese Men of War and the harpoon tail of the giant stingray. A great treat was night swimming. If we were in luck the water was phosphorescent. Tiny organisms which had absorbed sunlight clung to our bodies and the surface of the water turning them luminous and sparkling. Sometimes we made expeditions out of town to a deep green pool in a river where we loved to splash and dive the whole day long. We shared the cool water with hovering butterflies. Astonishingly once a soft duvet of white butterflies landed on me, covering me from head to toe. It sounds like a fantasy but how could one make up such a story? I was wearing a lime-green dress which must have attracted them.

Bicycle was our chief mode of transport. We were very lean and fit from the amount of exercise we took. We thought nothing of cycling from Oyster Bay along the coast road to the centre of town and back again. Our bikes, unceremoniously dumped at our destinations were never stolen or vandalised. I recall one marathon bike ride I did with some friends in the heat of the day. My inner thighs were rubbed raw and my face, neck and chest were so badly burnt they came up in blisters. We did not use sunscreen and my aged skin is now paying a heavy price.

We seldom made tourist trips. When our parents travelled for pleasure they did not take us. This may have been to save money or because they thought we made enough journeys to and from school. Mum did one special trip with Harriet to the Ngorogoro Crater. This was a fantastic treat which might have caused sibling rivalry was it not for the fact that it was a prelude to being sent to England alone to finish her schooling. I was, however, taken to two historic places within reasonable reach (only a few hundred miles) of Dar: Bagamoyo has connections with the Arab slave trade. In Swahili the name translates as "Lay down your Heart" which is so poignant considering it was the last stop for these unfortunate captives on the caravan route. Here they arrived after their exhausting march from the interior knowing that soon they would be exhibited for sale in the slave market in Zanzibar. It was on the doorstep of the church in Bagamoyo that Livingstone's faithful servants finally laid down his body and few possessions. We also visited the island of Zanzibar. We found Zanzibar instantly exotic and different from the African towns we knew. The Arab Fort and the royal palaces were the oldest and most elaborate buildings we had ever seen in Africa. And we had never smelt a place so sweet. The outdoor markets were stacked with spices and cloves which scented the warm air.

I associate Dar with burgeoning sexuality and volatile adolescent passion. Clothes had become extremely important. I think I was more fashion-conscious than either Harriet or Jane. Mum's homemade creations were no longer acceptable. Fortunately there were some competent tailors at hand. I loved choosing fabrics from the Indian shops and taking them to be copied from designs out of glossy magazines. There was not much anyone could do with my dead straight hair but I was not prepared to let Mum have a go any longer. So I was allowed to have it cut professionally. I can't remember how much pocket money we were allowed but it was very little because there was little to spend it on. Our parents paid for the club subscriptions. Our favourite rendez-vous was the Cosy Café in the centre of town where there was a limit to the number of ice-creams and soft drinks we could consume.

In fact, our teenage pursuits were very innocent. I did not feel at all rebellious at this stage in my life. What was there to rebel against? I suppose everyone in the ex-pat community knew everyone else so my parents were not critical of the company we kept. Either we were ignorant of drugs or they were not available to us. As far as alcohol was concerned we were occasionally allowed to drink beer which appeared to satisfy us. At this stage, a relationship with an African or Indian boy would certainly have caused a scandal. But since the ethnic groups were still highly segregated, and the opportunities to meet each other as social equals rare, this situation did not arise.

I have been told that I broke a few hearts, but as a typically self-absorbed teenager I have forgotten which hearts these were. I recollect more clearly the occasions when I was humiliated or rejected. I still blush at the memory of a malapropism I made when I was flirting with a boy on the beach. I had been reading too much Jane Austin and boldly suggested that we had a tete à tete. Unfortunately it came out as teat a teat. The minute I spoke I knew I had got it horribly wrong. My most miserable experience was getting dumped by an older boy called Andy Ransford who went to boarding school in South Africa. He probably got tired of what he regarded as teasing. Our kissing, fumbling and hand-holding was done at the cinema, and at teenage dances. I drew the line from the waist down from a fear of pregnancy rather than virtue.

Mum was always available to soothe our heartaches and to facilitate our social rounds. She kept open house for our friends, organised barbeques on the beach and drove us to dances at night. There surely must have been some unhappy or discontented teenagers amongst our acquaintances and friends but I don't remember any. There would have had to be something really bad going on to have been discontented in such a paradise.

Chapter 13

School

To our great relief our parents did not send us to school in England. Instead they chose a convent in Kenya. As it was, the journey was almost as long and arduous as it would have been to travel overseas. Even though I was sent off to boarding school at the age of five, I do not remember being homesick. This may have been because the journey from Biharamulo to Nairobi was so thrilling. The anticipation started with the ritualistic packing of our black tin trunks. Mum used to spend half the night before departure sewing name tapes onto the prescribed items of uniform which were typed on a sheet of paper which had to be stuck to the inside of the lid. Navy blue gym slips, divided shorts for games, white aertex shirts, white socks, pants, dressing gown, pyjamas and a jar of malt. We found it hard to sleep for excitement. We had to leave before light and travel 200 miles in the back of a government lorry on a bumpy dirt road to Bukoba which was situated on Lake Victoria. The only part of the journey I disliked was the picnic meal. We had a picnic box made of metal which heated up everything inside so that the bread and butter and even the hard-boiled eggs smelt and tasted rotten and metallic.

This part of the journey was never without incident. A tree might have to be removed from the road. During the rainy season the lorry tended to get stuck in mud or stall when crossing a flooded ravine. We might have to stop while a troop of elephant crossed the road. Motors were very basic and frequent stops were required to allow the radiator to cool, to change the fan belt, to swap tires. We would also stop to pick up sick Africans or pregnant women who needed to get to the hospital in Bukoba. On one occasion the lorry was flagged down by some agitated Africans who loaded a companion into the back of the lorry with us. He had been stung by hundreds of wild bees while up a tree trying to get honey out of a hive. He was laid out unconscious on some sacks. To our horror he began to swell up before our eyes. His arms, legs, face and neck ballooned out. His breathing became loud and harsh. We were terrified this man was going to burst with a pop. He was dropped off at the hospital in Bukoba where he was given an antidote which brought him back to life and to a normal size.

The next stage of our journey was on one of the lake steamers, the Usoga or Rusinga which plied their way round all the major lake ports. The first time I went to school, we were accompanied by Mum. Thereafter, we made the journey alone although there was always a volunteer adult acting as escort on the boat. We were also joined at this point by more boys and girls who were going to the various boarding schools in Kenya. These sizeable old steamers carried white passengers in first-class accommodation and Africans in steerage with trading goods. We loved the boat trip, especially when the captain was in a good mood and allowed us to pull the horn when we approached ports. We liked squeezing into the tiny airless cabin with its round porthole. We felt very grown-up taking meals in the dining-room and had to behave ourselves if the escort was present. We spent hours leaning over the rail looking down at the Africans below with their live chickens and picnics and general air of enjoyment. We stopped at Entebbe and Jinja in Uganda before disembarking at Kisumu in Kenya.

Then came the climax of the trip: the train journey from Kisumu

1st class on lake steamer

to Nairobi. When the Imperial East African Company had proposed a railway across Kenya it was dubbed in parliament a lunatic line and deemed unrealistic. However, the company took the risk, raised the finance and succeeded in building it against all the odds. These included termites which ate the wooden sleepers, accidents and disease which decimated the Indian work force and two fearsome man-eating lions at Tsavo which devoured 28 workers. Despite the myriad obstacles the lines were laid mile after mile. The railway took twice as long to build and cost twice as much as predicted, but for better or worse it changed the history of Kenya. And there we were, children of the Empire, forty years on, riding across some of the most spectacular scenery in the world.

How musical the names of the stations sound in my ears to this day. Londiani, Kericho, Nakuru, Gilgil, Naivasha and Fort Hall. I can conjure up the chuffing rhythm of the train on the tracks which seemed to match the beating of my heart. It was fun to wave out of the windows at the little *totos* standing transfixed at the track side. Stations were like mini bazaars where traders would crowd round the windows selling bottles of sodas, burnt corn, chewing gum, bananas, meat stews and *ugali* (maize porridge). In these early days the floor of the Rift Valley, through which the train wound its way, was teeming with wild game. Herds of elephant, wildebeest, zebra, giraffe, buffalo, a variety of deer, leopards, lions and rhino (now almost extinct) roamed the land. When we chuffed past Lake Nakuru the water was pink with flocks of flamingoes.

There was no need to pay for expensive safaris to see wild animals. We just had to keep our eyes open.

By this time a larger crowd of European school children had assembled. We were assigned in fours to compartments which we called dog carriages. Each carriage had its own door and steps to the ground. When we had squabbled for the top bunks we wolfed down our boxed meals. If we had a lazy or inattentive escort we got up to all sorts of mischief. We leaned right out of the windows either to shout at friends in adjoining compartments or to watch the engine which was visible like a snake's head when the tail of the train twisted in the opposite direction. Dad had cautioned us about the perils of leaning out of train and car windows with the story of a friend who had been blinded in one eye by a flying pebble. He would have been horrified if he had witnessed what we sometimes did when the escort was not looking. When the train slowed down, as it frequently did for a steep climb, some of the more foolhardy of us would climb down the steps and walk slowly beside the train until it picked up speed when we would jump back on in the nick of time. To my knowledge no one was ever left behind.

On one return trip from Nairobi to Kisumu some boys from the Prince of Wales School in the next compartment to ours played a very dangerous game which had frightening consequences. Towards the end of the journey as the train was passing through a vast area of grassland full of wild game, the boys started throwing lit matches out of the window to see if they could stay alight until they hit the ground. The odds of this happening were very low but as mischance would have it, one did not extinguish itself and fell on dry grass alongside the track. It was incredible to see how quickly the flames ignited the dry undergrowth. The fire crackled and burnt with speed turning the bush into a lake of molten gold. We passed too quickly to see wild animals stampeding in panic. But from the distance we watched in awe as the sky turned a deep red like an angry sunset. But it was no sunset. What we were seeing was the reflection of an unstoppable bush fire. We felt sober as we melted into our compartments. I don't believe anyone reported this incident. Certainly I never spoke of it again.

My parents chose a convent rather than a secular school like Limuru or the Kenya High School for us to go to in the belief that we would be well educated, strictly brought up and secure. In fact, this was something of a false prospectus, but I was very happy at

Loreto Convent Msongari which turned out to be an eccentric school. One approached it by a winding road lined with jacaranda trees. It was an imposing double storey white building with a tiled roof. A series of open arches gave the ground floor the feel of a monastic cloister. The school was built round an internal quadrangle with an interior chapel at one end and a detached assembly hall at the other. Some time during my school days a larger-than-life white marble statue of the Virgin Mary was erected on a plinth in the forecourt. The crowned Virgin held a sceptre in one hand and the baby Jesus in another. This resplendent figure was surrounded by a rosary in the form of white balls on a chain. A long narrow avenue between glossy-leaved coffee bushes linked the Convent with a Catholic boys' school called St Mary's which naturally was strictly out of bounds. The grounds were extensive and included tennis courts, a hockey pitch, gardens at the back and front and *bundu* beyond. There was a small river well to the right of the hockey pitch that ran towards the road. It too was strictly out of bounds.

I have a vivid memory of my first day at school. Harriet, who had already been at the school for a year, skipped merrily off to find her dormitory and friends while I was invited by Mother Superior, a wrinkled old crone in a white robe and black veil, to come and see the kitchen garden which was at the back of the school. She took me by the hand and led me away. Little did I know that this was the cue for my mother to leave. I am sure she wept as she did so. When I realised she had gone without saying goodbye I felt very upset and betrayed but quickly recovered from this setback. It was a question of sink or swim and I must have taken a decision to swim. Besides, our regimented convent life did not leave much time for reflection or lamentation.

During our early years we slept in Fort School in dormitories of twenty beds with twenty lockers for our meagre possessions. Mother Pauline, a sweet and gentle personality was in charge of us. She had a helper called Tanya who mended our clothes and tied ribbons in our hair. In lieu of a daily bath we had to give ourselves strip washes in the wash room which included using the flannel under our armpits and "down there." We would get help with our weekly baths only when very young. When we moved up to pre-prep and prep the dormitories got smaller until, as seniors, two shared a room. We were trained to dress and undress modestly under dressing-gowns or in cubicles. The nuns were very strict and neurotic about all this which I much later realised was a sign of sexual repression. I would like to think that I have liberated myself from the shame of nakedness but have to confess that, even now, I cannot bring myself to strut around naked, as everyone else does, in the changing room in my health club. I do my dressing and undressing as I did as a child, and still do on a public beach, by wriggling into my under-clothes under the concealing folds of a towel or top.

Our regime was ruled by bells. We were woken at 6.30 a.m. When we had donned our uniforms we had to make our beds with hospital corners. Then the Catholics went to morning chapel while the Protestants gathered in a corridor. This was followed by breakfast in the refectory. The whole school, including staff attended morning assembly in the hall. This was the occasion for important announcements, or denouncements if someone had got into trouble. The Catholics, who were in the majority, would worship in the chapel while the Protestants used the tail end of a parquet corridor. Here we would kneel on the hard floor while a senior would read a lesson or lead us in the Lord's Prayer.

We were certainly made to feel inferior for not being Catholic. It did not escape our attention that in the Christmas tableaux the Virgin Mary was always pretty little Catholic Maureen O'Halloran. The Head Girl also tended to be Catholic. Inevitably, many of us heathens went through a phase of wanting to convert. At one stage my parents wisely allowed me go to Catholic chapel. For a year or two I wallowed in the ritual and ceremony. I was enchanted by the obligatory head veil which was secured by an elastic band and fluffed out over the shoulders. I was thrilled by the genuflections and the dipping of the finger in holy water to make the Sign of the Cross. The pinnacle of ambition was to sport a coloured ribbon across the chest. These were for the good girls who undertook duties in chapel or sacristy or read lessons. The chapel was decorated with statues of the Virgin, Stations of the Cross, and a huge crucifix over the altar. There were images too of bleeding hearts and an image of Christ with a crown of thorns on his head and blood coming out of his hands and feet. The altar was covered with lacy linen and, except during Lent, there were candles and flowers in profusion.

Christ's Corridor, as the Protestant parquet strip was known, could simply not compete. My ambition was to get confirmed so that I could get a present of a silver cross and chain and wear a pretty white dress with white shoes and socks and of course the delectable veil. I don't think I was aware of the bridal references at this point. The confirmations which took place every year seemed very grand affairs. A Bishop or important priest officiated and there was a tea party afterwards. After confirmation you could go to confession once a week. You would kneel in the wooden confessional and in a whisper tell your sins to the male priest who sat half hidden behind a grill. I longed to partake of this thrilling experience. Just the thought of it gave me a frisson. According to my Catholic friends, the only punishment they ever got was to say a dozen Hail Marys even if they had confessed to having impure thoughts.

My longing to be a Catholic convert was temporarily so intense that one year I even volunteered for the annual retreat from which Protestants were exempt. This was a three-day event designed for prayer, contemplation, self-discipline and the purification of the soul. We abstained from talking, were not allowed sweets or puddings and our reading was confined to religious books. When I begged my parents to allow me to convert to Catholicism they said I could do so if I still felt the same when I reached eighteen. By the age of twelve I had come to the conclusion that it was much cooler to be a Protestant and reverted to Christ's Corridor in a spirit of defiance. The objective was to get there first and slide all the way down to the windows at the end. I now made it my business to tempt my Catholic friends to share titbits of forbidden food, to communicate via notes and to read naughty books during their retreat.

There was no discrimination when it came to Corpus Christi. This feast day was the highlight of the convent's religious calendar. Corpus Christi, which is the feast to commemorate the Holy Eucharist, took place on the last Sunday after Holy Trinity in late May, or early June. Preparations started weeks before the great event. The object was to decorate the avenue which linked the two schools with a carpet of flowers representing religious symbols. Every flowering tree in sight was stripped of blossom, every flower in the kitchen garden was removed and exotic blooms were purchased for the occasion. The precious piles of mauve jacaranda, assorted roses, orange marigolds, white lilies, pink oleander, red cannas, maroon fuchsia, purple bougainvillea, blue agapanthus, yellow mimosa and scarlet poinsettia drenched the air with a sweet cloying scent. Then, on Friday and Saturday the hard work began. Designs were chalked onto the ground ready to be packed full of petals. The senior classes were in charge of the more intricate designs while the junior classes did the borders and fillings. Many a tear of frustration was shed, knees were bruised from kneeling to the task, frantic last-minute errands were run to find new blooms, prayers were said to stave off rain or wind. One year I was in the team responsible for the Holy Ghost in the form of a white dove. Another year our team got a prize for our monogram I.H.S made from orange marigolds and dark green leaves. The summit of privilege was to create the Loreto school badge in red and white with touches of green. The four quarters contained a cross, two hearts and an anchor. This honour was given to the seniors. Sunday was heartbreak day. Down this glorious scented carpeted avenue processed a line of priests in full regalia swinging incense thuribles, followed by troops of nuns, visitors and children. The patterns were scattered, the blooms crushed and the holy symbols obliterated. All in the time it took to walk one-third of a mile.

Chapter 14

The Nuns

I have no recollection of the lay teachers with the exception of Mary Vail, the PT teacher. She was young and attractive and was engaged to be married which we thought very romantic. I am told that I disgraced myself on one occasion by bending down and feeling her muscular calves. The nuns I will remember to my dying day. The old Mother Superior who took me to the kitchen garden on my first day must have died or retired because it was her successor whose image is strongest: Mother Scholastica had one blue eye and one green eye which we believed gave her second sight into our misdemeanours. I found her rather chilling. She might well have been a sympathetic character, but her position of authority and the punishments she metered out turned her into a feared figure. Punishments ranged from slight to severe. We might be put with our back to the class in the corner of the classroom, or made to stand outside the door for the duration of the lesson. Worse was being made to stand in public view by the birdbath in the quadrangle. We would be kept in for detention during free time to do hundreds of lines or copy chunks out of the gospels. I got my fair share of the range of punishments. Doing penance in the quadrangle was far and away the most humiliating. For bigger sins we could be gated which meant missing treats and days out. The final resort was expulsion. This sanction was used with absurd abandon. Quite often girls who were expelled were allowed back, especially if they happened to be Catholic.

Mother Peter Claver was another formidable figure. She had very blue bulging eyes (probably due to a thyroid condition) and enormous buck teeth which gave rise to her nickname *meno* which means teeth in Swahili. One had to be careful around her because she had a temper. She would stretch her upper lip over her prominent teeth, her chin would quiver and she would let rip. She taught Latin and History and was a hard task mistress in the classroom. She did not brook inattention and would swoop down and slash a wooden ruler across our knuckles. On one occasion she slapped a friend of mine across the face. We used to titter about her having a man's name. In fact, she had chosen as her named saint a rather apt figure. Peter Claver was a Spanish Jesuit priest who was sent as a missionary to Cartagena in 1610. There he dedicated himself to relieving the plight of the African slaves who were being shipped across the Atlantic in large numbers.

Mother Cyril was a favourite. She was so small and round that when she sat on a stool her feet did not reach the ground. She taught science and was affectionately known as *Squirrel*. Mother Florence (*Flo the Buffulo*) had bad breath which was a barrier to intimacy. Mother Hyacinth taught hockey as well as geography. She had a yellow weather-beaten face and delighted us by tucking her habit into her rope belt and streaking up and down the hockey pitch. Mother Philippine was young and beautiful despite the disguising severity of the veil. She was very musical and taught me singing and violin. We all worshipped her. Even the nuns with feminine-sounding names were named for males. Hyacinth of Cracow was a Dominican missionary in the 13th Century. Cyril and Florence were also male saints. I really wonder why these pioneering women did not choose to be named for female saints. There were a few they could have settled for. Mother Scholastica was an exception in choosing to be named after the sister of Benedict.

In hindsight, I have much sympathy for these spinster women who took the veil, made vows of obedience and chastity and served God by teaching hordes of ungrateful and privileged white girls. It never occurred to me that they might be missing their families in Ireland. In our day I don't believe they were allowed to go home on leave. I heard an enlightening story recently about *Meno*. After receiving a visit from one of my contemporaries, (by then in her forties), Mother Peter Claver begged her forgiveness for having been so strict. She explained that she had been brought up in an academic family which had left her with a zeal for her pupils to excel at lessons. As she was nearing the end of her life she was obviously seeking absolution.

The sisters of the Institute of the Blessed Virgin Mary was a pioneering religious order for women founded in 1609 and modelled on the Society of Jesus by the Yorkshire woman Mary Ward for whom a mass was said once a year.The Irish and American branches of the order have recently amalgamated under the name IBVM Loreto. In recent times the Catholic Church in Ireland has been reeling from shocking revelations of mental and physical abuse perpetrated by monks and nuns on children entrusted to their care. During our time there was no sadism at Loreto Msongari. When there was bullying it was done by pupils. I have a nasty feeling that I was a bit of a bully when in my teens. I know that I was the ring leader of a gang that threw a girl with the unfortunate nickname of *Dotty du Potty* into a patch of giant stinging nettles.

In such a closed community friendships were passionate and the popular girls in the in-groups could be cruel and spiteful to outsiders. Sometimes girls were sent "to Coventry" and not spoken to for days. Conversely, the close-knit friendships we formed substituted for the families who lived so far away. We were quite a European Union what with Swedish, Italian, Norwegian and Belgian girls. But we were strictly all white. Loreto nuns were running separate schools for Africans and Asians but Msongari did not open its door to other races until independence.

For many of us the convent was a second home. I believe that the nuns understood about home-sickness. They encouraged the older girls to mother the juniors and they were indulgent about birthday celebrations. Every birthday girl was greeted at breakfast by a pile of little presents hidden beneath a cover of flowers and topped with a birthday cake. I can't imagine where our cakes came from as our parents were so far away but some arrangement must have been made. They also relaxed the rules for any of us who had to stay at school during half term or some of the holidays. They would let us make our cubicles into houses where we would have midnight feasts. And we were allowed to have picnics and we could go swimming in a neighbouring private pool.

The fact that fifty years on I am still in touch with a group of my class mates is testimony to the strength of the bonds of friendship between us. My best friend at the convent, Ingrid Stjernsward, is still my closest friend. How could it be otherwise after sharing the ritual of shaving our legs (leaving a lot of bloody nicks) and rolling our first cigarettes? My sisters and I did not see our parents at all during term time. The only way to be in touch was by letter. Letter writing was an obligatory ritual Sunday afternoon activity. Until we were seniors our letters were censored by the nun in charge. If they contained seditious material, spelling mistakes or ink blots they had to be done again. Not surprisingly they followed a bland set formula which told only half the story.

Dear Mum and Dad,
I hope you and the dogs are well and happy. I am very well and happy. I came top of the class in history this week and came third in the test of the capitals of the world. We played hockey against the Kenya High School Second Eleven and beat them 3-2. We were allowed orange segments in the interval. We saw a film of Laurel and Hardy in the hall last night. It was very funny. Laurel's feet got stuck in a bowl of cement. The Irish Father is coming back to sing Irish songs. I hope he does Mama's Little Baby Loves Shortnin' Bread again. Please send me a parcel soon. Love from Julia.

The plea for a parcel was a code for *I am hungry*. I got into great trouble when I wrote in one letter that I was starving. I was made to tear it up and start again. But it was true. The food was disgusting and inadequate. When we were not doing lessons or homework we were doing sports, gymnastics, hockey, netball and tennis. We expended huge amounts of energy, there was never enough to eat and I was constantly hungry. As juniors, the only supplement we could get our hands on was malt, listed as medicinal, which we would bring to school in our trunks. Mrs Shepherd-Smith, the matron, used to spoon out the precious malt each morning to a queue of girls who waited outside her surgery.

The thought of Mum's parcels makes me smile. They were so badly constructed it was a wonder they arrived at all. I got one with the head of a toothbrush sticking out of a corner. Nevertheless her food parcels containing Ryvita biscuits, tinned butter and a jar of bovril were most welcome. If the contents were not confiscated I would stuff my face until I felt bloated. It was sheer heaven. As I got older I found ways and means to fill the hunger hole. Stealing from the lay staff dining-room was one. Bribing one of the servants to slip me the odd piece of bread and jam was another. The African servants who did the cooking and housework were Catholics and could sometimes be persuaded to provide the odd bit of food in exchange for a holy picture. Mathias was in charge of the dining-room. He was a Mkamba and had his teeth filed into points. We were told that this was to enable him to eat more easily in case he got lock jaw. It is more likely to have been a tribal adornment. We were scared of Mathias who could be moody. There were mango and avocado trees and mulberry bushes in the grounds and when in season the fruits would provide a little extra nourishment. But picking the fruit was stealing which was a deadly sin and so one had to be very circumspect. It was a gang operation. Someone was posted as lookout while someone tall was required to hoist the avocado picker on her shoulders. English raspberries and straw-berries don't hold a candle to a sun-ripened mango or avocado.

It was useful to be friends with a day girl to whom one could give money to purchase a Crunchie or Mars bar. Our parents gave us a small amount of pocket money each term for necessary purchases like toothpaste, shampoo or stamps. This was kept under lock and key and doled out on request. But like prisoners in a cell we got adept at finding secure hiding places for extra money and illicit possessions. In my last year at school a few of us managed to organise a secret tuck shop. A delivery van would drop provisions out of sight down the avenue. We paid the Indian shopkeeper for tins of condensed milk, sardines, chocolate bars, custard cream biscuits and dry-as-dust pink meringues and then sold the surplus at a profit. The effects of feeling hungry as a school girl have never left me. I still gobble my food. I am unable to leave a crumb on my plate and the thought of going on a diet or being deprived of a meal makes me feel panicky.

We became adept at leading double lives at Loreto Convent. On the surface we were goody goodies. The discipline in the classroom would be the envy of any teacher today. We stood up when the teacher entered or left the room. In response to the greeting, "Good morning girls" we would chant in unison: "Good morning Mother Cyril." Interruptions were only allowed if you raised a hand to ask permission to speak. Whenever we passed a nun in a corridor we were supposed to give way and to drop a curtsey. We were ticked off for bad deportment. Our hands and fingernails were inspected for dirt. We did not swear or use bad language. We were expected to be truthful and honourable. We knew the Ten Commandments by heart. Breaking these commandments could lead to eternal damnation. Even small sins were shameful. Sex was a forbidden fruit and not to be contemplated outside of marriage.

Below the surface we managed to hoodwink the nuns and have a lot of fun. Much of this took place at night in the toilet cubicles which we nicknamed the *pollies*. Here by torchlight we would gossip and play cards. Here too, rather bizarrely, the more diligent amongst us would swot up on lessons and test each other. I spent many an absorbing nocturnal hour reading *Katherine* (disguised in brown paper) by Anya Seton. It seems extraordinary now to think that this rather well written historical romance with its veiled references to sex and passion was the sexiest reading material to hand. In private, our language and conversation would have shocked the nuns to the core. We speculated endlessly about what they looked like under their robes. We wondered whether they shaved their hair or just hid it. We imagined that they took baths in tent-like garments so as not to see their own "down theres." We exchanged smutty ditties such as, "Lady of Spain I adore you. Take down your pants I implore you." We were competitive about wearing bras and menstruating which rather tellingly was known as "the curse." We were constantly breaking bounds, including crossing the forbidden river.

During our teens romance and sex were seldom far from our minds. There were the boys of St Mary's, tantalisingly close and there were fleeting opportunities to meet them. They used our concert hall for their plays so we were able to ogle them as they came and went for rehearsals. We were also allowed to watch the final performance. I recall one play they did was *The Barretts of Wimpole Street*. Protestant church, to which we walked in a crocodile every Sunday, was another convenient venue. We seized every chance, even an appointment with the killer dentist, to visit town. There was Corpus Christi and the occasional sporting or musical event. The first step in a rather curious courting ritual with a boy was to get hitched which was formalised by the mutual exchange of bracelets made out of giraffe hair. These were made and sold to tourists and were easily available. Dropping and picking up SWALK (Sealed with a Loving Kiss) letters from an arranged drop (a rock or hollow tree) without being seen was thrillingly dangerous. Meeting to kiss, and fondle was even more dangerous.

Inevitably, Ingrid and I were caught kissing boys in the coffee plantation. The disgrace was public. Mother Superior was implacable and we were duly expelled from school. We had to endure days of agony and tears while waiting for the arrival of our parents who had to drop everything to travel to Nairobi. I can't believe that they treated the misdemeanour with the same seriousness as the poor nuns, but they must have donned sackcloth and ashes and pleaded effectively because our punishment was commuted to detention and we were allowed to stay on. When we were seniors private dances were organised out of school and so the nuns lost some of their control over us. We wore very pretty dresses with tight bodices and full skirts on top of layers and layers of net petticoats which we stiffened with flour and water. When we twirled and twisted and turned upside down to the rhythms of rock and roll and the jive, the petticoats showed to perfection.

School life was full of excitements. One term there was the snake scare. A huge black mamba had been spotted by the river. We were not allowed out until it had been found and killed which took some time. Another term we had a polio epidemic. Poliomyelitis or infantile paralysis, as it was sometimes called, was a common disease at this time and affected hundreds of thousands of people in the world. It was a viral infection which could spread from person-to-person. When it broke out at school there was much talk of a boy called Ian Bumpus who was lying in hospital in an iron lung. I could vividly imagine him encased in a contraption that looked like a suit of armour in which he could not move. We all knew that polio could cause paralysis for life because many of the African beggars hobbling on crutches in Nairobi were it's victims. We were all immediately put into quarantine and lined up in rows in the forecourt. A team of medics moved methodically down the lines brandishing their hypodermic syringes filled with pink serum. Squeamish pupils began fainting where they stood. Had I been a fainter, (which to my chagrin I was not) this would have been my moment. The vaccine had only very recently been developed. Happily the one used on us and the more refined ones which followed, have resulted in a global eradication of polio.

Another very frightening and dramatic occasion was a personal one. We were disturbed to receive a letter from Mum to say that she was flying to England to have an operation for breast cancer. Until then I had never known her take to her bed or complain about her health. She explained that the surgeon would remove a lump and that there was nothing to worry about. She promised to buy us some new clothes while she was about it. It was now that the words of the Sufi came back to me with such clarity. Although my sisters and I didn't talk much about Mum's cancer amongst ourselves we sensed it was serious. I am not sure that we knew that cancer was potentially life-threatening but subconsciously I must have worried that Mum could die because in her absence I had a vivid nightmare in which Mother Superior summoned us to her office. There she sternly told us that Mum had died, and as there was no money left we had to swim across Lake Victoria to get home. Dodging crocodiles, we swam for our lives. As we crawled, exhausted and gasping onto the shore, I woke up crying and panting. In the event, Mum returned safe and sound and laden, as promised, with clothes and presents. In characteristic fashion she made light of the disfiguring mastectomy she had undergone.

My parents considered that I was well educated by the time I left the convent in 1957. I did too: in fact, I thought I was a star. I had passed the Lower School Certificate (Cambridge Board) in 9 subjects, five of these with distinction. I had learnt how to play the violin and reached quite a high grade on the piano. I led the altos in the school choir. Harriet, Jane and I had been photographed in the East African Standard after winning an inter-schools singing competition. There we were, looking smug in our school uniforms with our feet in the plié position and our hands piously clasped at waist-level under the caption, *The Singing Sisters*. I played full back in the hockey team and shooter in the netball team.

Singing in the choir

But my star fizzled out when transported to England. After attending my new school, Huyton College in Liverpool for only a few weeks I realised that most of my learning was meaningless. Granny Phillip's handy aphorism that "all that glitters is not gold" was apt enough. We had been taught all our subjects by rote. It amazes me now to think that I could recite the whole of St Luke's Gospel by heart. Somehow I had even learnt maths by heart without grasping a single principle. I couldn't make head or tail of physics or chemistry. My piano grades were worthless because I could not sight-read or improvise. I had mastered French grammar but could not speak a word. In History and English I could spout what I had learnt but my analytical and creative faculties were non-existent. It took me years to free myself from counter-productive learning habits I had picked up at the convent.

But there were positives too. I have not always worked wisely but I have always worked hard and for this I must thank the nuns. Mother Philippine left me with a great love of church music which I indulged later by singing in church choirs. I know how to sew, mend and even to smock. I also learnt the importance of courtesy and good manners from the nuns who placed such a premium on these virtues. These are so ingrained in me that on occasion I have wished I felt freer to curse and swear. A school that fosters life-long friendships is a happy school. I was happy at the convent and remember it with deep affection. Rules and regulations were the order of the day, yet somehow there was a sub-culture that fostered originality and autonomy. I have never felt this way about any subsequent institution in which I have been involved. Loreto Convent, Msongari left a recognisable stamp on us all.

Chapter 15

Mau Mau

Much of my time at the convent was spent during a period of intense unrest in Kenya. Although the nuns did a good job of protecting us from the realities of the outside world we did acquire a partial understanding of the situation. As far as we were concerned the Mau Mau revolt (1952-1960) was a native rebellion against British colonial rule. The baddies were Kikuyu terrorists who were threatening white settlers in a bitter dispute over land and power. The Mau Mau rebels were creating havoc largely in the Highland areas. They were stealing and maiming livestock on white farms, burning houses and farm buildings and murdering fellow blacks as well as whites. Terrible stories were in circulation about the violent oath ceremonies they were conducting to force loyal servants and farm helpers to turn against their employers, even to murder them. All white women were given arms and taught how to use them in self defence. Many of the men joined the Police Reserve or the Kenya Regiment. Curfews were introduced and volunteers provided as much protection as they could to farmers on isolated farms. It was thought that the insurgency would be crushed in no time but it continued year after year, sucking in 50,000 British troops. There were so many soldiers in Nairobi it looked more like a military garrison than the rather ramshackle town we knew.

Against this backdrop our daily routine at school continued almost unchanged. Out-of-bounds limits were more strictly enforced. It became harder to wangle trips to town. The school gate was padlocked at night and watchmen were placed on guard. One night there was a commotion when shotgun reports were heard, followed by a rattling of the gates and shouting. We jumped into each other's beds where we remained shivering until a nun passed through the dormitories in an effort to reassure us. I don't believe we ever learnt what the commotion was about. Scary incidents like this as well as rumours and stories would periodically disturb the cosy pattern of our school life. Perhaps because a child was involved I can recall the horror story of a Mr and Mrs Ruck and their six-year-old boy who were hacked to death by terrorists armed with *pangas*. This was in 1953 when I was twelve years old. I was told another haunting story by a farmer's daughter. She described how pregnant Kikuyu women who would not swear the oath had their babies cut out of their tummies while they were still alive. After hearing that I slept with a hockey stick under my bed.

During the Emergency, my parents seriously considered sending us to boarding school in England. In the end they decided to stick it out while taking the precaution of getting us guaranteed places at Huyton College in Liverpool. Perhaps this decision was influenced by our pleadings because we dreaded being sent away from the convent almost as much as we dreaded the Mau Mau. It was not until my left-wing days at Oxford University that I formulated a more balanced picture of the Emergency. The uprising was the result of long-simmering political, racial and economic tensions between the Kikuyu and the white settlers. Most of the territory appropriated by white immigrants in the Highlands of Kenya belonged to the Kikuyu who were restricted to 2000 square miles while the settlers occupied 12,000 square miles. Some natives were permitted to have *shambas* on white farms in exchange for their labour. Supposedly tenant farmers, they were in effect agricultural labourers and began to bitterly resent it.

Many Africans fought in the British Army in both world wars and rightly considered, on their return, that they deserved a better deal. The hatred the Kikuyu began to feel for the interlopers was harnessed by educated leaders whose attempts to get political and social concessions were continually thwarted by the white minority reluctant to give up its power. Viewed through the eyes of Africans, Mau Mau leaders like Stanley Mathenge and Dedan Kimathi were heroes and freedom fighters rather than terrorists. The rebels did use extremely dirty and disagreeable tactics, in particular against their own people but they paid a high price in their struggle to regain control of their own country. 26 Asians and 32 Europeans were killed during the Emergency compared to some 2,000 Africans. Thousands more were interned. Only very recently has the full extent of alleged British brutality during the rebellion begun to emerge through government reports documenting systemic torture, starvation and death of Africans in detention.

Although the last Mau Mau leader Dedan Kimathi was captured in 1956, the state of Emergency remained until 1960. By this time I had long since left the convent. But if the white settlers won the battle they ultimately lost the war. The Mau Mau rebellion forced the British government to realise how untenable colonial rule in Kenya was. The political demands of the Africans began to be met and preparations for independence were started. *Uhuru* eventually came to Kenya on 11 December 1963 after 68 years of British rule. Jomo Kenyatta who had been imprisoned during the emergency was voted in as President.

My parents lived too far away for it to be feasible to go home for half-term breaks. We had either to stay at school or with friends in Kenya. One half term during the unrest I went to stay with a friend called Jenny Banks, whose parents had a farm near Molo in the Highlands where some of the worst atrocities were being committed. I imagine everyone must have been on full alert but all I can remember of this visit was the fun we had. The Banks family was very keen on riding and we spent our time dashing about on ponies, attending gymkhanas and practising jumping in a field. I was on the farm with Jenny on 2nd June 1953, the day Princess Elizabeth was crowned Queen. The previous year the Princess had been staying with her handsome young husband Prince Phillip at Treetops Hotel in Kenya when news of her father's death reached her. The couple had to curtail their holiday and rush back for the funeral of George VI. Partly because of this the Kenyans had a proprietary feeling towards the new queen and celebrated her coronation with gusto. A holiday was declared on the farm and whites and blacks all joined together for a sports day. We competed in sack races, and tried not to drops eggs out of spoons. We ducked for apples in troughs of water and sprinted and hurdled. The prizes were all won by the farm boys who were natural athletes. For another half-term Camilla Kopperud's Norwegian parents invited me to a large house and extensive farm near Nairobi. A holiday with another friend called Jill Gould has stuck in my mind because I disgraced myself by riding a toddler's tricycle through a glass door.

The Stjernswards were the most generous hosts of all. Hans and Viveka were Swedish and incredibly glamorous. Viveka was a blond beauty who looked like a model when she wore her fifties dresses with their tight bodices and full skirts cut on the bias. These she made herself having done a dressmaking course in Paris. She was gentle and sweet-natured. She was the daughter of Ingrid Lindstrom who, with her husband Gillis, always known as *Bwana Samaki* (fish) because of his protruding eyes, were pioneer white settlers in Kenya. When Nellie and Jos Grant came out to Kenya to settle in Njoro they found that their nearest neighbours were the Lindstroms. Nellie and Ingrid became close friends. The Lindstroms had four children, while the Grants' only child was Elspeth Huxley. Ingrid Lindstrom features in Elspeth's book *The Flame Trees of Thika*. There is also a rather fanciful portrait of her in Karen Blixen's *Out of Africa*:

> She had all the broad bold insinuating joviality of an old Swedish peasant woman, and in her weather-beaten face, the strong white teeth of a laughing Valkyrie. Therefore does the world love the Swedes, because in the midst of their woes they can draw it all to their bosom and be so gallant that they shine a long way away.

Hans was a dark Swede with beetling black eyebrows. He had a volatile temperament and buckets full of charm. He came out to Kenya as a bachelor and worked on the Lindstrom farm and in a canning factory run by Nellie Grant. Inevitably he fell in love with the beautiful Viveka. They married, acquired a farm of their own at

Ingrid, Louise and Philippa

Rongai and produced three daughters. It was the oldest daughter Ingrid, named for her grandmother, who became my best friend and partner in crime at the convent. She had two pretty younger sisters Louise and Philippa who was a toddler when I first went to the farm. Until I went to stay at Rongai I knew nothing of the legendary white settlers like Karen Blixon, Galbraith and Berkeley Cole, Denys Finch Hatton, Lord and Lady Delamere or the Happy Valley crowd. I had not heard of Elspeth Huxley whose reputation as an African writer was becoming established. It was through my friendship with the Stjernswards that I subsequently became friends with Elspeth and Gervase Huxley in England. Their only son Charles and I were up at Oxford together and much later I spent happy and interesting weekends with them at their home Woodfolds in Wiltshire. When Charles married his first wife – Frederica – Christopher was asked to stand as Godfather to their first son, Jos Huxley. The sequence of these relationships snaked all the way back to Rongai.

I took it for granted at the time, but now realise how open-hearted and generous the Stjernswards were to have me to stay in the way that they did, especially during the Mau Mau. European settlers in Kenya were famous for their hospitality. Farmers mostly lived miles from a town and miles from each other. They relied on each other for assistance, support and entertainment and consequently kept open house for relatives, strangers and friends. Life was never boring with

Ingrid Lindstrom and Elspeth Huxley.

the Stjernswards. They were very popular and people were always popping in and out of the house. Hans was a great tease and the house was full of noise, laughter and unruly dogs. Never a day passed without some crisis or other on the farm. Viveka was a competent farmer. She was suited to the life and loved it. I was greatly impressed on one occasion when I watched her perform an operation on a turkey which had an obstruction in its throat. She grabbed the turkey by the legs, pinioned it on her knees, slit its throat with a razor, pulled out the lump of whatever it was, and sewed up the wound. Unbelievably, the turkey strutted off as if nothing had happened.

The Stjernswards had proper dinner parties with several courses and good wines. It was with them that I ate my first artichoke. They were highly amused by my hopeless attempts to deal with it before showing me how to nibble at the tender base of each leaf. From their conversation I realized that they moved in a different and more posh social circle from my parents who mostly consorted with government service families. They owned large tracts of land and talked about racing, hunting and polo. They attended Horticultural and Agricultural shows in Nakuru. It was through them that I first heard about the Muthaiga Club and the famous Norfolk and Stanley Hotels in Nairobi. Curiously, in quite another context and time of my life, I became friends with Lyn Fuss, the daughter of Jack Block whose father had built up both these hotels in the early days. Jack Block's father, Abraham Block was a Lithuanian Jew who had come to Kenya via South Africa as a penniless young man in search of opportunities. By working incredibly hard, turning his hand to multiple activities and taking financial risks, he made a fortune and established a social position for his family in Kenyan society.

Sadly, the Stjernsward marriage did not survive a move to the UK. Hans went ahead at the end of 1962 to look for a job while Viveka kept the farm going. By the time she left Kenya to join him the marriage had fallen apart. At least I was able to resume my friendship with Ingrid who had turned into a blonde bombshell and whose time was largely spent fending off love-stricken suitors. Despite living in Britain for more than forty years, she still has the luminosity, humour, resilience and originality that I associate with our African childhood.

Chapter 16

Home

Home, as we were led to believe, was not Africa but England to which we were removed every three years or so for long leave. Our first port of call was usually St Anne's Road in Liverpool, the home of our maternal grandparents. It didn't feel a bit like home to me though. The house was approached by a driveway and had a large garden and orchard at the back. It consisted of two stories, an attic and basement. My chief memory of the house is the perishing cold. The rooms with their high ceilings were filled with Victorian furniture and objects we had never seen before: a rocking horse, gas fires, a grandfather clock and a barometer. But these did little to compensate for what we were missing.

We were depressed by the grey skies and dismal weather which compared poorly with the hard bright African light and storms that announced themselves with claps of thunder and zig-zags of lightening, before releasing torrents of hot rain that perfumed the parched earth. We hated the restriction of the woollen clothes and lace-up shoes we had to wear. It was hard to appreciate the common-or-garden sparrow when we were used to rainbow coloured rollers. We didn't like being told to behave like nice little English girls rather than savages and to refrain from speaking Swahili. The reality was that we felt like aliens and were desperately homesick for Africa, our dogs, our friends and our freedom. I was not the sort of child who would normally have spent hours on a rocking horse lulling myself into a trance of boredom but that's a feeling I can still recollect.

Did my parents also suffer from culture shock on their home visits? I imagine so, especially when we returned in 1948 – after a long absence – to a Britain recovering from the war. Society was changing fast with the introduction of the NHS, comprehensive education and a growing stock of council housing. But there was still high unemployment and widespread poverty. Large parts of Liverpool were heaps of bomb-damaged rubble and the inhabitants looked drab and dreary to match. Mum came back from shopping one day in a rage. She was wearing a leopard skin coat in which she always looked dashing. Rationing was still in existence and she had spent hours in a long queue of complaining women with whom she had suddenly lost her patience. She left without the article she had waited so long to purchase.

On the other hand they were relieved and overjoyed to find the whole family intact. Uncle Harold and Auntie Evie were still alive. Mum's siblings Molly, Denis and Leslie and our cousins Victoria, Sandra and Mark made frequent visits to the house to see us. Our favourite relative was Auntie Molly who was a mean card player and taught us a vicious game of Racing Demons. What we didn't realise at this time was that her husband, the glamorous Bobby Cope was drinking heavily. When the family firm Cope Cigarettes was taken over by Gallaghers he lost his job which did not help. The family had moved to Oswestry in Wales where Molly was keeping the family afloat running an egg-packing business. Victoria was sent away to boarding school but I was sad to learn recently that her life at home was not happy because her father was very unkind to her.

In their house they had a pretty occasional table that had a curious Liverpudlian history. The former owner had been Joseph Bruce Ismay, the chairman of the White Star Line which built and owned the Titanic. Ismay set sail with the ship on its maiden voyage on April 10th 1912. When the Titanic sank he took refuge in a lifeboat and was picked up the by The Carpathia. He may well have wished that he had gone down with the ill-fated Titanic because on his return to Liverpool he was vilified and shunned. He also had to attend a Board of Trade inquiry in London. He was held in such contempt for being a coward that he sold up and left Liverpool. Molly acquired the table in an auction of his possessions.

Denis had taken part in the Italian campaign for which he was mentioned in despatches and awarded the OBE. But his marriage to Anne Harrington was falling apart. The bottom had fallen out of the cotton business so he was busy looking for alternative employment. He eventually bought the kipper-curing company Orrel Brothers in Peel, Isle of Man in partnership with his younger brother Leslie. For Denis, work was only a means for making money. As soon as he had acquired enough he retired to lead an idle ex-pat life on the Island of Majorca. There he met Lucy Joad who became his second wife.

Lucy's father was the famous (or in some quarters infamous) Cyril Edwin Joad. He was a brilliant philosopher, writer and broadcaster who had become a national figure on the *Brains Trust*. Unfortunately he was also a risk-taker and took pride in the fact that he cheated, whenever he could, by travelling on the railway for free. In April 1948 he was caught without a valid ticket on the Waterloo-Exeter train and was prosecuted and fined. Not only were his hopes for a peerage dashed but this extraordinary folly put an end to his career, his place on the *Brains Trust* and his reputation.

Leslie had ended the war as an intelligence officer in India where he had spent much of his time in hospital with jaundice and hepatitis. He was more fortunate than Denis in that he had an enduring and secure relationship with his pretty wife, Auntie Connie who was sweet-natured and loving. Their children Sandra and Mark were our playmates in Liverpool. Sandra was clearly Granny's favourite and we got tired of hearing how good and brainy she was!

Memory plays lots of tricks. In my case it tends to blank out unpleasant or painful memories. I find it almost impossible to recall La Sagesse, the convent school we temporarily attended during our leave in England. All that I can be sure of now is that it made me utterly miserable. I got into trouble for crashing into a girl during a gym class and breaking her nose. No-one paid any attention to the fact that I had damaged a front tooth. Even though it wasn't loose it felt as if it was. Gradually it turned grey as the nerve died. I was self-conscious about it until at the age of seventeen it was filed and capped. I also cut across a teacher who took her revenge by constantly picking on me. Mum rose to the occasion, as usual, aided by the knowledge of African witchcraft she had learnt from Hans Cory. We constructed a rudimentary figure out of wax. Next she laid a curse on it which she did with much waving of arms and mutterings in Swahili. We reduced the figure to a melted blob by warming it up with matches. "Now I guarantee" she promised, "that no matter what she says her words will have no more power over you." And she was right.

There were, of course, many new and interesting experiences. We loved travelling on trams and buses. Liverpool trams were called green goddesses on account of their colour. They had rather uncomfortable seats and made a clackety-clack noise as they rattled along the tram lines. No one worried about child molesters in those days and we often travelled around by ourselves. Shopping never failed to enchant. The big department stores made the African *dukas* look cheap and tacky. Even the grocer's shop in Aigburth Road with its pavement stalls piled high with plums, strawberries, apples and pears made our eyes pop. My first view of winter snow was a magical moment. One morning the garden was transformed into a fairy wonderland by a soft pure blanket of snow and glittering icicles. We rushed out after breakfast, made a snowman and had snowball fights. Then we went tobogganing in Sefton Park with a wooden toboggan and tea trays.

Homesick though I was, I had to admit that an English Christmas with all its rituals was superior to an African one. A proper Father Christmas holding court in the grotto at Sackler's was more authentic than one of my father's friends in disguise. The gift you received was accompanied by a cuddle which would be tantamount to paedophilia today. It was wonderful fun to be able to buy proper presents with the money we had saved up, instead of having to make something. The best treat of all was the pantomime. *Cinderella* was one I particularly remember because the men playing the Ugly Sisters were grotesquely funny and vulgar. I loved joining in the hissing, booing and shouting – "Oh! Yes it is … ..Oh! No it isn't".

Decorating the house was good fun too. Branches of holly and mistletoe were draped over pictures and on the mantelpiece and home-made paper chains were hung across the ceilings. Ten days before Christmas a huge spruce tree was brought into the sitting-room. Granny Phillips watched us closely with her beady little eyes to make sure we didn't break the delicate glass balls that were kept in boxes lined with tissue paper. We had to be careful too to place the clip-on candle holders at a safe distance from the silver tinsel. The wrapped presents under the tree added to the almost unbearable anticipation. We were allowed to stay up late for carol singing in the music room.

When Christmas day arrived at last there was church to be got through before we could light the candles and tear open the presents. This ceremony was followed by a gargantuan lunch of turkey with all the trimmings and brussels sprouts which we detested. When we hadn't got room for another morsel the plum pudding was carried into the dining-room engulfed in blue brandy flames. I didn't actually like the texture or taste of the pudding or the brandy butter but it didn't matter because the point was to look and see if one had been lucky enough to find the hidden silver sixpence. Crackers had great appeal for the unanswerable riddles and the paper hats which made the grown-ups look so very ridiculous. At three o'clock we listened to the Queen's childish crystal voice as she read out her speech on the radio. We couldn't wait for it to end so that we could play charades, Racing Demon and Up Jenkins which involved sleights of hand and a coin. There was considerable moaning and groaning on Boxing Day when we were kept in until we had finished our thank-you letters.

Our customary sojourn to London was a further mixed bag of treats and duties. On the negative side our holiday was punctuated by visits to dentists, doctors and occulists. The only time I was ever in hospital as a child was when I had my tonsils and adenoids removed at St Mary's Paddington. With the best of intentions my parents arranged for me to be in a private room. Although they visited every day, I was miserably lonely for a whole week. I can see myself standing at a window watching school children playing far below and wishing I could join them. To add insult to injury I missed going to *Peter Pan* which made me sadder than anything else.

We did not much enjoy our duty visits to see Dad's aunts, uncles and cousins – with three exceptions: we liked Charlotte Beardmore who had been brought up by Austin and Frances Dobson. Known to everyone as Cousin Shaddy she was a dedicated social worker and my father was devoted to her. We were intrigued by her flat because it was filled with a bizarre assortment of objects like rugs, trolleys and electric toasters which she had won by answering quizzes in magazines. We also loved having tea at the Ritz with Uncle Bernard's wife Margaret and tea at the House of Lords with Christopher Dobson. Both were formal occasions for which we had to dress up. We were over-awed by the ambience of the Ritz where a band played while we were served cucumber sandwiches, scones and dainty cakes on tiered stands. Tea was followed by a picture show on a wide screen in a large plush cinema in Picadilly Circus. Walt Disney's wondrous *Living Desert* was the first nature film I ever saw. The coarse white cups and saucers in the House of Lords were not comparable with the porcelain plates of the Ritz but the lavatory more than made up for it. We thought the flowered toilet bowl set in a huge wooden box with its pull chain was hilarious.

And then there was CULTURE. Dad was only too conscious of what we were missing out on in Africa so we were subjected to a regime of museums, art galleries, churches, monuments and concerts. Dad was a patient and knowledgeable guide and did his best to spice things up. We were always welcome at 50 Albemarle Street. This was the headquarters of the famous publishing house John Murray. The entrance hall had a black and white checked floor and a beautiful cantilevered staircase. Original cartoons done by Osbert Lancaster adorned the walls above the staircase. On the first landing stood a bust of Lord Byron who was the house of Murray's most famous author. John Murray VI (known as Jock) would meet us and take us into the middle drawing-room. I had supposed that my father and Jock made friends at Oxford but John Murray VII, who became a friend of mine at Oxford, claims that my mother had dated Jock before my father came on the scene.

Jock was a man of great charm and affability who always wore a spotted bowtie and red braces. He would treat us as if we were the most important people he knew and show us some of the house's famous archive exhibits. These would be brought up from a linen cupboard in the basement. Sir John Moore's Corunna pistols were of interest in the light of our family myth. We were intrigued by Bryon's tiny boot which had a lead sole for the correction of his distorted foot. (Dad's stock present to all of us at Christmas was a book of the latest Osbert Lancaster cartoons. It occurs to me now that his appreciation of Lancaster was probably fostered by Jock Murray). John Murray VII still owns 50 Albermarle Street which looks much the same but he sold the publishing firm and donated the archive to the National Library of Scotland.

Our favourite expedition was to Madame Tussaud's which, in addition to life-like models, had an intriguing basement full of peepshows and distorting mirrors. The Tower of London which offered an exotic combination of Crown Jewels, haunted prisons and sinister execution spots came a close second. As a child I found CULTURE wearisome. In the long run though, my father's efforts to educate us were not in vain: years later I discovered I was a historian. I was a poor student at Oxford because I found the history course too dry and academic, but when I began teaching history to school children it all fell miraculously into place. My writing career began with short history plays written for my pupils to act out in the classroom. I then surprised myself by loving the research for my first published book; *The Children of Charles I*. For my third book; *Children of the Tower*, I described the lives of twelve children who had been connected with the Tower over the centuries. I know my father was pleased when he read the foreword by Digby Raeburn, Resident Governor of the Tower.

I first met Julia Dobson when she visited the Tower to gather material for Children of the Tower. At the time I was struck with her knowledge and her scholarly approach to her subject. You may be sure that all her facts are historically accurate. The book, though, is much more than a catalogue of Tower events. The author's inventive approach and her lucid and graceful style make the book a special pleasure to read. It is written in the first place for children but, like all the best children's books it will appeal equally to grown-ups.

Getting to and from our various destinations was often more fun than the destination itself. It was a thrill to ride on the top of a double-decker bus and to travel on the Underground. Fellow passengers were friendly and polite and it was common practice for children to offer their seats to adults. When we were in London we would stay in a boarding house in Bayswater which was central and cheap. This run-down and shabby area had once been highly fashionable; in fact, Westbourne Grove had been dubbed the Bond Street of west London and boasted Whiteley's Emporium. The department store of William Whitely, nicknamed the "universal provider" proved such a success that in 1925 he completed the handsome deco building in Queensway that still bears his name today. We used to take the manually operated lift to every floor where we would admire everything from buttons to bathtubs. Eventually, in the 1980s Whiteley's was boarded up but thankfully, not destroyed, because of its preserved status. I would never have imagined that some thirty-five years later I would have ended up living in this area with my own family. In the last twenty years we have seen Whiteley's re-opened as a shopping mall, houses in the neighbourhood smartened up and returned to single occupancy; and the Paddington Basin development. But I am glad to say that Paddington and Queensway have retained something of their former louche and cosmopolitan atmosphere.

One of our home leave London rituals was the Sherlock Holmes trail. Dad tried hard to communicate his passion for Sherlock Holmes to us children. In my case he partially succeeded. I found the detective stories, especially *The Speckled Band* and *The Hound of the Baskervilles* deliciously spine-chilling when I read them for the first time. We would visit 221b Baker Street, the site of the digs Holmes shared with Dr Watson. Life has a strange way of coming full circle. Some years after my father died, my husband, Christopher, became Chairman of Abbey National. In those days the bank's handsome art deco headquarters incorporated 221b Baker Street. I was astonished to learn that letters from people of all ages and nationalities addressed to Sherlock Holmes were arriving at the bank on a regular basis. These were written as if to someone who was still alive and in business. "Would the great detective fly to the Unites States (all expenses paid) to solve the mystery of some missing jeweller?" "Dear Sherlock Holmes" wrote a school girl, "My teacher at school says that you do not exist and never have – only in fiction. Would you please write and tell me if this is true." I have some sympathy with this correspondent. As a child I found it hard to distinguish reality from the fiction, as I suspect my father did. Tongue-in-cheek Abbey National colluded in the fantasy. A part-time function of one of the secretaries was to reply to the letters, regretting that Sherlock Holmes could be of no assistance as he had retired to Sussex to cultivate bees.

Inevitably Christopher, who is a great bibliophile and collector of first editions, caught the Sherlock Holmes bug and accumulated a collection of Conan Doyle's books. He also became acquainted with Conan Doyle's daughter Dame Jean Doyle. In 1999, to commemorate Abbey National's 150th birthday, Christopher commissioned the sculptor John Doubleday to make a statue of Sherlock Holmes. It is a fine ten-foot bronze figure of the beaky-nosed detective in deerstalker hat, and long cape. He is holding a pipe in his right hand. The local council refused permission for the statue to be erected outside the bank so it was placed with great fanfare and ceremony at the entrance to Baker Street tube station.

From Baker Street Dad took us through the historic landmarks: Sherlock Mews, James Taylor & Co (Holmes' shoemakers); the Cafe Royal in Picadilly where Holmes was attacked in *The Adventure of the Illustrious Client,* The Criterion Bar where Watson first heard that an eccentric medical student called Sherlock Holmes was looking for a roommate; the Sherlock Holmes pub in Northumberland Avenue with its Dickensian atmosphere and exhibits and finally, a typically English meal of roast beef at Simpson's in the Strand where Holmes and Watson liked to dine. Doubleday very generously gave Christopher a small scale replica of his statue of the great detective. Whenever I see it in the study I am reminded of my father and wish I had been more responsive to his passion. I can now appreciate his efforts to immerse us in English culture. It was not his fault that it left us a bit cold. The problem was that home to us was not England but Africa.

Chapter 17

Dislocation

Whether or not we thought of England as home, we had no choice but to accept that it was when we left Africa in August 1957. This was the year my father chose to retire (prematurely) from service overseas. He made the decision partly because his health was deteriorating, and partly because he knew that with independence approaching his job would be one of the first to be taken over by an African. It was to prove a dramatic dislocation for all of us in different ways. Having trained in later life as a psychotherapist and having written a book about loss and grief, I can now see that we were all grieving the loss of our friends, animals, work and social life as well as Africa which had seeped into our bones. We flew home by plane. On landing I got a severe nose bleed which was so profuse that a vein in my nose had to be cauterized by a doctor. I now view this nose bleed as a symbolic protest.

Last photo taken in Africa

My parents rented a flat in Sevenoaks while they searched the Kentish countryside for a house to buy. In the flat below ours lived a woman who had a grown-up daughter with Down's Syndrome. It shames me to confess it but I found this profoundly depressing. Money worries came to the fore for the first time in our lives. We had never really thought about money in Africa. There was a limited amount to buy and we had what we needed. Much of this was provided by the government. We were not at all materialistic or competitive. But now money became an endless subject of conversation. We were told to watch the pennies, switch off the lights and to mind the pips on the telephone. Mum understood our misery and tried to cheer us up with the gift of racing bicycles with gears and drop handlebars. We would have been thrilled with these in Dar but in England heartily disliked pedalling up and down steep hills wrapped up in cumbersome duffle coats which we knew at once were unfashionable. And how we felt the cold. The flat had no central heating and the gas fires were inadequate. We suffered colds, sore throats and chilblains which were painful and itchy at the same time. So there we were – cold, friendless and lost in a strange land. No wonder we felt sorry for ourselves.

To make matters worse, we were sent to boarding school in Liverpool. Places had been kept open for us at Huyton College during the Mau Mau and my parents felt obligated to send us there. Harriet had already been and gone from the Sixth Form. Huyton, which is no longer in existence, was the Cheltenham College of the north. It had a good academic record, and extensive sports facilities. It was largely patronized by girls who lived in the surrounding counties of Cheshire, Lancashire Wales and Northern Ireland. Both Jane and I hated it. Being ex – colonials and southerners we felt like fish out of water. The conventions and regulations were restricting, the lack of privacy oppressive and the uniform unattractive. I used periodically to lose my voice for no apparent reason which I now recognise as a sign of unbearable stress. The only member of staff I can remember with any clarity was Miss Oates who was a very good history teacher. The one real friend I had was a maverick called Sally Smeeton. If the school still existed and I was told to find my way around it I would get lost.

My parents must have felt equally dislocated but I was too wrapped up in my own concerns to pay much attention. Dad could have got a civil service job without difficulty but decided not to seek re-employment. This was a mistake because after a life of toil he had far too much time on his hands to worry about himself. He had a bad back, asthma and incipient emphysema which greatly curtailed the quality of his life. He became a hypochondriac, relying more and more on my mother who became increasingly housebound in response to his neediness.

As women often do, Mum adjusted to her new life better than Dad. The purchase of a permanent home was a turning-point for us all. It was a comely well-proportioned red-brick house which dated from the 18th Century. It amused me to tell my friends the address which was: Priors, Jackass Lane, Keston. Keston was a genuine village with two pubs, a post office and a tobacconist situated just inside the green belt. Yet we were very close to London whose highlights we were beginning to enjoy. Mum became an ace at cooking on the Aga which warmed up the kitchen. She remained as hospitable as always, entertained liberally and kept open house for our friends. She also took control of the extensive garden. When it became apparent that Dad's pension was not going to cover the family's living expenses and our educational needs, Mum set to and became an intensive poultry farmer. Two broiler houses were erected in the orchard by the garage. Rearing hundreds of chickens in crowded artificial conditions, force-feeding them and then catching and crating them for slaughter was a horrible and physically demanding way to make a living. We helped as best as we could in the holidays but the brunt of the hard work fell on her.

We had returned in time to join a family celebration for the Golden anniversary of Grandpa and Granny Phillips. This took place over our first Christmas. We stayed with all the uncles, aunts and cousins in the Tyn-y-Wern Hotel in Llangollen. We went for long walks and played endless games of charades. This reunion provided a good chance to get to know our distant family better. Grandpa died in the following year. A few years after this Granny Phillips and Molly purchased a small house in Keston so as to be near us. When Granny died in 1967 her house was sold and Priors was divided so that Molly could live in one half with my parents in the other. This was an ideal arrangement for the two sisters who were the best of friends. They played bridge, did the Times crossword and shared a Meals-on-Wheels run.

Now and again the Australian Ambassador, Ruth Dobson came to visit us and Dad was simply delighted when her sister Rosemary,

Alec and their three children Lissant, Ian and Robert came to the UK in 1966. Alec was running the London office of *Angus and Robertson* publishers at the time. He also went to night school to learn printing. On their return to Australia Alec was appointed Publishing Director of the National Library. In addition, he and Rosemary devoted themselves to their private *Brindabella Press* which produced high quality Australian poetry (including some of Rosemary's) with wood engraved illustrations These slim volumes are now rare and expensive collector's items. If only I had had the wit to buy them as they came out. Contact with the Australian branch of the family has happily continued through Lissant Bolton who has spent a major part of her career as curator of the Oceania Department in the British Museum.

I married Christopher Tugendhat on the 8th April 1967. The story of our married life is for another time. All I need to do now is to clarify a few reference points for this account. When I married Christopher he was a journalist on the Financial Times. In 1970 he became MP for the Cities of London and Westminster. In 1977, when he was appointed Commissioner to the European Union, we moved with James and Gus to Brussels for eight years.

Both my parents got ill and died while I was living in Brussels. I went over to see them whenever possible but it was never enough. My father was the first to die. After several miserable experiences in hospital he got Mum to promise to keep him at home where thankfully he died in his own bed on the 18th June 1981 at the age of 74. He was cremated in a meagre and impersonal service in Croydon Crematorium. After his death a light was extinguished in my mother. Her cancer came back and spread from her back to her brain. When she was taken into Guy's Hospital, in New Cross, I took James who was ten years old to visit her. Although Mum was bald and incoherent he appeared not to be too affected. He hopped into a wheelchair and began racing it up and down the corridor. This was the only moment of light relief in the last night-marish months Mum spent in hospital. Although it was clear that she was dying, it was difficult to talk to anyone in charge and somehow we were unable to stop her dreadful cancer treatment and get her back home. On one occasion she walked out into the streets in her dressing gown and was not rescued for hours. For twenty years after Mum's death Molly would repeat the incident to me with anguish. The hospital informed her of what had happened in these words, "Mrs Cope we have to tell you that we have lost your sister."

My sisters at last managed to bring Mum home to die on the 19th May 1983, at the comparatively young age of 71, worn out by the rigours of Africa, factory farming and the effects of smoking. James and my mother had been so devoted to each other that I thought it better to spare him the funeral which took place in the same ghastly Croydon Crematorium as Dad's. This, I now realise, was a mistake because he needed a grieving ritual as much as I did. Although Mum's relationship with Gus was not as close because of our move to Brussels it would have benefited him too.

When we returned to Priors for the simple wake which had been kindly organised by our neighbour Rhona Shave we found a pile of paper napkins embellished with the injunction to Have a Nice Day on the table. This sent my sisters and me into a giggling state of collapse. Rhona Shave had already become a legend in our family. When her husband Donald was alive, but in failing health, Rhona was much more affectionate to her dogs than her husband. She and my mother had an arrangement where they would collect each other from Heathrow after trips abroad. On one occasion when Rhona was there to meet my mother, the conversation went like this:

"Oh! There you are Rhona. How are you?"

"Fine thanks, Barbara."

"And how are the dogs?"

"In great form I'm glad to say."

"And Donald?"

"Dead I'm afraid."

Molly was devastated by my mother's death. And we in turn were devastated by her death in 2001. She outlived all her siblings. As the years passed it began to bother me that we had dispatched my parents with so little ceremony, without any plaques or memorials in an ugly, anonymous crematorium which we had no desire to visit. While I was writing my book *How to Approach Death* I decided to organize a re-interment service for both my parents and for Molly. After much coming and going this took place at Keston Parish Church on the 9th February 2008. The kindly Canon Springthorpe officiated. James read out the tribute I had written to my parents which at the risk of repetition I shall quote in full:

My grandparents Kenneth and Barbara Dobson worshipped in this church, helped with the parish magazine and lived down the lane, so it could not be a more appropriate place for this commemoration service. Today we have been given a special opportunity to transform the grief we have been carrying for so many years into a celebration of their remarkable lives. They spent the first 25 years of their marriage in Africa. There they pursued their careers in the colonial service in Tanganyika with dedication and integrity – and at a considerable cost to their health.

Kenneth who was the son of missionaries and a long line of public servants could not have done anything petty or shoddy if he had tried. He was thoughtful, dutiful and wise. Barbara was extrovert, generous, humorous and a tremendous life force. Relatives, friends, colleagues and all who met them would have agreed that they were good people. Family was very important to them. They fell in love at first sight and remained devoted and loyal to each other all their lives. They were supportive and loving parents and doting and involved grandparents. Though they died at a comparatively young age for our time we hope and trust that some of their virtues, beliefs and goodness have passed down to us. We are fortunate to have memories and role models which we can cherish and be proud of. I am sure that in our turn we will bring our children and grandchildren here to remind us of Kenneth and Barbara Dobson.

It was a great comfort having Lily, my first grandchild with all her passionate liveliness at my side. Jeremy Isaac spoke about his beloved grandmother Molly. After the service a box of symbolic earth taken from the crematorium and Molly's ashes were interred in front of this pretty country church. Their names and dates are inscribed in the memorial book which is kept inside the church. And I am content with their final resting place.

Gradually Harriet, Jane and I adjusted, acclimatized and went our separate ways but there is no doubt that our lineage and our African childhood influenced our life choices. The chief lesson Harriet gained from her experience of coming to England alone was self-sufficiency. She learnt to cope with her life and problems on her own. She is so potty about animals that it caused no surprise when she followed in Mum's footsteps by studying agriculture at Seale Hayne in Devon. She then worked for Cadbury's and on various farms until she married Toby Roxburgh who was a publisher. For a few years they lived in New York where their twins Grant and Belinda were born.

When they moved back to the UK they bought a house close to my parents who became deeply involved in their lives. Harriet acquired a cattery where she housed cats during their six months of enforced quarantine. In 1987 they sold up and bought a farm on the Isle of Islay where they still tend cows, a bull, sheep, pigs, cats and horses. In addition to rearing animals for slaughter they rent out holiday flats and organise pony trekking. They scrounge grants from government and EU sources. The RSPB pays them a small sum to allow Canadian geese to winter on their land. Despite the relentless hard work needed to keep their heads above water, they would not want to live anywhere else in the world.

If it was not for the wind and rain Islay would be close to paradise. Pastures and peaty moorland sweep down to the wide sandy beaches off which orcas, seals and dolphins cavort in the sea. Buzzards and other birds of prey surf the air pockets. Three species of deer, otters and hares inhabit the hills and forests. The attractive island towns have not been allowed to sprawl and are concentrated in strategic areas. The numerous whiskey distilleries with their long white buildings are distinctive landmarks. The Scottish writer Iain Banks devotes six pages of his book *Raw Spirit* to the Roxburgh family and Ballivicar Farm. I like his description of Harriet whom he describes as wonderful, "and even more ruddy-cheeked than her husband, with a great, pealingly infectious laugh and a neat ability to control a fully loaded quad bike while remaining undistracted by a small platoon of accompanying dogs and children. She drives a mean chariot too (they have a chariot made from plywood, an old car axle and what looks like bent scaffolding poles which gets lashed onto the Clydesdale and pulled around the fields with Harriet and a bunch of bouncing, whooping, yelling children aboard). Harriet is usually to be found tramping across the farmyard with a bucket of something noisome or just plain smelly swinging from each arm."

Of the three of us Jane most resembles my father. She is highly intelligent and thoughtful. She was so unhappy at Huyton College that my parents took her away and sent her to Bromley High School as a day pupil. Unconsciously perhaps, she has followed family precedent in a number of ways. She went to St Andrew's University like our great-aunts Mildred and Dorothy. There she read ancient and modern history and won the history prize. She followed this by winning an English Speaking Union scholarship to Bryn Mawr in the United States. After a year she decided that academia was not for her and, like Austin Dobson and great-uncles Bernard and Alban, she entered the civil service. She kept her career going after her marriage to the solicitor John Sharman and the birth of her two boys Richard and Andrew. She worked in the Ministry of Public Buildings which eventually became the Department of the Environment. She transferred to English Heritage in 1984 ending up as Acting Chief Executive. She has been associated with a range of heritage bodies: the Heritage Lottery Fund, the Architectural Heritage Fund, HMS Cavalier (Chatham Trust) the Royal Artillery Museum Woolwich, The Chatham Historic Dockyard Trust, Bexley Heritage Trust, and the Vivat Trust. Her distinguished career was recognised in 1997 when she was awarded a CBE.

I like to think that I am most like my mother in personality and appearance (though not so beautiful alas). My significant career choices have been characterized by a conflict between the frivolous and the serious. Half of me has longed for fame, fortune and fun. The other half is drawn to good works. I hated Huyton College but managed to acquit myself well, acquiring enough good A levels to gain a place at Lady Margaret Hall, Oxford. There my social life blossomed at the expense of my academic studies. I made friends for life, fell in and out of love, experimented with sex and partied like crazy. In short I squeezed every drop of fun from life. 1960-1963 was a marvellous time to be a student: social mores and conventions were breaking down, the contraceptive pill was on the market and hippies were the rage. After Oxford I took myself off to New York for a year and found employment as assistant to Cranston Jones who ran the Modern Living page on Time Life. While I was working for him Time Life ran a cover entitled London: The Swinging City which I helped to research. After travelling by Greyhound bus as far west as Chicago and down to Mexico I returned to London and a job on the Arts page of a new glossy magazine called *About Town* which was part of Michael Heseltine's publishing empire.

But then the missionary gene kicked in and I turned to teaching, first in Grey Coat School for Girls, then a Comprehensive school in Peckham and finally in a private preparatory school for girls called Glendower. I loved teaching and think I had a talent for it. I only gave up after Christopher became the MP for The Cities of London and Westminster when the combination of constituency duties, public life and teaching became untenable. Luckily I was able to turn to writing which fitted around the births of James and Gus and over the years I have written 11 books for children under my maiden name. In order of publication these are:

> *The Children of Charles 1, The Smallest Man in England, Mountbatten: Sailor Hero, Children of the Tower, They Were at Waterloo, The Ivory Poachers, The Tomb Robbers, The Animal Rescuers, The Wreck Finder, Danger in the Magic Kingdom, The Chinese Puzzle.*

None of them made me much money but I rate the history books, especially *The Children of Charles I* and *They Were at Waterloo*. I think the Crisp twins adventures would have been more widely sold if they had been more energetically marketed. I was pleased to learn from my Public Lending Rights returns that for years the adventures were being read in public libraries. Although I have searched high and low I have never found any of my books in second-hand book shops. The adventures were poorly produced and probably perished but I am surprised not to have stumbled upon any of my non-fiction titles which were hardbacks.

On our return to the UK from Brussels I had a crisis of confidence about my ability to write. I had some rejections for the first time in my writing career and decided with singular lack of courage and perseverance that I was a sham and put down my pen. To compensate I spent many years training to be a systemic psychotherapist and ended up working part-time for both my training institutions – KCC and Westminster Pastoral Foundation. At the same time I ran a private practice from home with colleagues with whom I had trained. I worked with individuals, couples and families presenting with a variety of problems.

I managed to overcome my creative demons in 1990 when I wrote under my married name *What Teenagers Can Tell Us About Divorce and Stepfamilies*. This was followed by *The Adoption Triangle, Living with Loss and Grief* and *How to Approach Death*. The only one which has bombed is the last one which is not surprising considering the subject. From 1993-2002 I was a member (and from 2000 Deputy Chairman) of the Human Fertilisation & Embryology Authority which took up a lot of my time, taught me a huge amount and in the last two years of my tenure gave me considerable grief. Give and take a little I do not believe that Austin Dobson and his moralizing wife Frances would disown me.

Addendum

In January 2011 Christopher accompanied me on a return trip to Tanzania. I went with a great deal of misgiving. My memories of my African childhood were happy ones. I was afraid that I might discover that I had been living in an imaginary paradise. Fifty-four years had elapsed since I had been in the country. Perhaps there would be nothing recognisable left. My overall view of the whole African continent had been coloured over the years by the media's negative images of starving children, natural disasters, gun-toting soldiers, corrupt politicians and raped women. I did not want this jaundiced view to influence my judgment of Tanzania. I was also concerned about the effects of the population explosion that had taken place since independence.

In Dar we stayed in the Southern Sun, a high-rise modern hotel which had not been there in our youth. It opens onto the diminished Botanical Gardens which we had known well. The Askari monument (where we would meet up with our friends) was smaller than I remembered. Dad's Public Relations offices had been pulled down but the colonial government buildings on the waterfront are still standing. We drove around the immaculate grounds of the Gymkhana Club where we had spent so much of our time and where the main buildings are still recognizable. We had lunch in the Coral Beach Hotel in Oyster Bay which has become a very desirable residential area full of hotels, grand mansions and expensive cars. I identified where we used to live but not the house itself (if it is still standing) because every property is now blocked off by high stone walls and security gates.

Thanks to the helpful preparation of our friend, the publisher Walter Bgoya, our quest for the Hans Cory collection was a success. Walter provided us with a guide who took us first to the university which is shabby but situated in beautiful grounds. On reaching the library we were taken to a double steel filing cabinet where files of flimsy typescript notes were crammed. It was very moving to find several written by my mother. I also unearthed a letter written and signed by my father. They need to be microfilmed before they disintegrate. Our next stop was the museum which was shut to the public because of building works. We were met by the Principal Curator Dr Kweka and taken to a cupboard in a storage room where the Cory figurines were piled up in disarray. The collection originally numbered 900 but I doubt there was half this number left. Alas there are no resources to restore and catalogue this collection which will continue to moulder until it is too late. This is tragic because the tribal history recorded by Cory is in the process of being lost under the pressure of rapid urbanization. The Curator told us that all but a handful of the figurines had been removed from public view because mothers had complained about the phallic symbols. The figurines badly need to be catalogued, restored and united with the corresponding papers kept in the university library. I was glad that Hans Cory himself was not alive to see what had happened to his life's work which had been donated to the nation when he left Africa.

Before leaving for Mwanza we spent a day in Bagamoyo where the decay of some fine old Arab-style colonial buildings did depress us. A Catholic mission has made a sad little shrine in the remains of the church where Livingstone's body was laid to rest by his faithful servants. So much more could be made of these historic sites. During our flight to the west of the country we passed Mt Kilimanjaro wreathed in clouds and flew over vast tracts of empty land. In Mwanza we stayed at a new hotel called Ryan's Bay on Capri Point. It is run by an attractive Goan couple called Fortes – whose family has been in the country since 1928. The hotel is one of a number of their business interests. In colonial days there were so many families like the Fortes who kept the economy going but now they are the exceptions. The majority of Asians were forced out of the country after independence when their businesses and jobs (in public services) were taken over by Africans.

When we lived in Mwanza the town was small and contained. Today every surrounding hilltop with its characteristic topography of volcanic rocks embedded in rich green vegetation is covered with dwellings from shiny mansions to tin hovels. But it is still a really pleasant provincial town. I located the site of our first house on the waterfront. Lake Victoria is still sparkling and beautiful, despite the damaging pollution but the hippos, crocodiles, butterflies, monkeys and even dogs are gone. These creatures and a rapidly growing population cannot live side by side any longer. We could see the rusting roof of the old German fort which was our last house on the hilltop peeking out over some trees. But the way up was obscured by the cluster of skyscrapers and buildings lower down and we never reached it. We did a couple of boat trips on the lake and visited Saa Nane Island which brought back memories of the divine trips we had made as children on the government launch.

The highlight of the visit was the discovery of the cluster of graves that Dad had restored when he was DC in Mwanza. Finding the site was an adventure in itself. We drove north-east along the coast through countryside with *shambas* and herds of skinny goats and cattle, passed little towns with *dukas* and Africans sitting chatting by the roadside – which seemed unchanged since we were there. Finally, we reached Kagehyi which is now essentially a shady cemetery running down to the beach. We were surprised to find that it is an almost forgotten historic site full of memorials cared for by a toothless old curator and visited now and again by a handful of people like ourselves.

Me in Kagehyi Cemetery

The first memorial we reached was erected in the 1970s by a mission to honour the lives of some White Fathers and British missionaries who had worked and died in the region in the late 19th Century. Then we came to a concrete slab of a monument with a stone seat to honour the poor slaves who stopped at Kagehyi on their dreadful journey to Bagamoyo. Lastly, there were the two memorials restored by Dad. The walls of the cemetery and the concrete plinths no longer exist. The two rough headstones now stand in piles of rocks probably as they had been when they were first erected. One is roughly inscribed: F.B. 1875. I was saddened to see that Stanley had not taken the trouble to have Fred Barker's name inscribed in full. More trouble was taken to record the missionary: John Smith. MB. EDN.CMS. Died. 11, May. 1877. Aged 28 Years. The one in the middle has been constructed comparatively recently and contains a dedication in Swahili and English to Mabruki and five other native bearers who died in 1875 while Stanley was circumnavigating Lake Victoria.

On the way back we stopped at Bujora to visit the Sukuma museum which is a curious blend of Catholic mission religion and Sukuma tribal and royal traditions. The church, which is shaped like a large round African hut, is wonderfully decorated with colourful African art and tribal symbols. It contains a beautiful carving of an African Christ on the cross and a Sukuma woman as Mary.

On the penultimate leg of the trip we stayed in an elegant hotel called Plantation Lodge which is run by a German couple who used to farm coffee. It is half an hour from Lake Manyara where we saw flocks of pink flamingoes, sacred ibis, hornbills and crowned cranes. While we ate our picnic lunch vivid superb starlings, cordon bleus and speckled barbets came hopping down for crumbs. The following morning we set off early for the Ngorongoro Crater. From the rim we got a magnificent view of the crater floor with its subtle blend of browns and yellows and the silvery basin of Lake Magada. When we drove across the crater floor we had our fill of lions, fat zebras, graceful giraffes, warthogs, ostrich, a cheetah and wildebeest galore. On the way out we had a close encounter with a bull elephant who found us blocking his way when he wanted to cross the tarmac road. Elephants in the park now find it easier to use roads than to crash through the undergrowth.

The trip to these game parks certainly reconnected me at a visceral level with the physical essence of Africa: the smells, one's sense of insignificance in the vastness, the hard clear light. I was arrested by the weirdness of the sycamore figs, mahogany trees, sausage trees, and the tamarinds which as children we had scarcely noticed. It was, of course, wonderful to see the rich wildlife again but the wonder was a little tarnished by the tourist element of it all. The animals are still wild but the experience of viewing them on tarmac roads in 4x4s alongside a great many other vehicles full of tourists is tame. I envied my younger self who had been able to see these animals at my back door. It was hard to believe that I had taken the experience so much for granted.

Our last stop was Zanzibar. We stayed in Stone Town in the Serena Hotel. The town, its people, architecture and food is a rich mix of Arab and African. We were much more aware of being in a largely Muslim population. (Two exceptions to Tanganyika's peaceful history occurred in Zanzibar. There was a 45 minute bombardment by the British in 1896 when two palaces on the waterfront were destroyed. This was undertaken to ensure the installation of a particular sultan. The other was much bloodier. During the 1964 Revolution some twelve thousand Indians and Arabs were massacred by African revolutionaries. This prompted the mass exodus of the majority of Stone Town's non-African population. It was after this revolution that the uneasy union of Zanzibar and Tanganyika was created). The museums, housed in the old Omani palaces are rather quaint. We were really struck by how fair the commentaries were when describing slavery or colonial rule. Zanzibar is an exotic place beloved by tourists but once again we were sad to see how the public buildings and gardens built by the British are in decay. Maybe we are unrealistic in putting so much emphasis on cultural heritage. It is understandable that the Tanzanians have more pressing social priorities.

My apprehension about a return down memory lane had been unnecessary. For a start it had the important effect of restoring my faith in Africa (or at least this part of it). Tanzania is one of the few African countries unaffected by ethnic or religious conflict and has a population that takes pride in both its tribal and national identity. It was good to experience a country that was functioning and developing. Julius Nyerere's idealistic but economically disastrous socialist regime based on *Ujamaa* centralized villages was brought to an end in 1985. Since then the economy has been transformed with visible results that we could see for ourselves. There are slums but we did not see starving people. In fact the Tanzanians, who are generally slim and elegant look healthier than obese Europeans and Americans. I did not see a single crying child in two weeks. People were much better dressed and shod than in our day. My parents would have been amazed to witness the ubiquitous use of the mobile phone.

Of course there is some corruption, a lot of tedious bureaucracy and inefficiency, as well as a growing gap between deteriorating public services and free market enterprises. But on the whole, I think my parents would have felt uplifted by the progress made in the last fifty years. The Africans we met were as I remembered them – delightful and dignified. They are also curious and full of humour. For some reason they found the fact that I had been a *toto* in their country so many years ago extremely funny. Most of them had not heard of colonial rule. They are more interested in the present than the past. I think that is how it should be.

Lightning Source UK Ltd.
Milton Keynes UK
UKOW021104021211

183071UK00002B/3/P